MICHAEL DENNIS

Michael Dennis has been working for over twenty years as a Company Stage Manager, for companies that include the Royal Court Theatre, Donmar Warehouse, Royal Shakespeare Company, National Theatre of Scotland, Hampstead Theatre, Old Vic, Young Vic and Lyric Hammersmith.

He wrote the episode *A Grand Day Out*, starring Fionn Whitehead, for *Queers* (BBC/Old Vic).

Dark Sublime is Michael's first play.

Michael Dennis

DARK
SUBLIME

NICK HERN BOOKS

London

www.nickhernbooks.co.uk

A Nick Hern Book

Dark Sublime first published in Great Britain in 2019 as a paperback original by Nick Hern Books Limited, The Glasshouse, 49a Goldhawk Road, London W12 8QP

Dark Sublime copyright © 2019 Michael Dennis

Michael Dennis has asserted his moral right to be identified as the author of this work

'The More Loving One' from *Homage to Clio* by W.H. Auden, first published by Random House in 1960. Every effort has been made to contact the copyright holders and obtain permission to reproduce this material.

Cover image by Clayton Hickman

Designed and typeset by Nick Hern Books, London
Printed in Great Britain by Mimeo Ltd, Huntingdon, Cambridgeshire PE29 6XX

A CIP catalogue record for this book is available from the British Library

ISBN 978 1 84842 837 9

Dark Sublime was first performed at the Trafalgar Studios, London, on 25 June 2019, with the following cast:

KATE	Jacqueline King
MARIANNE	Marina Sirtis
OLI	Kwaku Mills
VYKAR/BOB	Simon Thorp
THE VOICE OF KOSLEY	Mark Gatiss
SUZANNE	Sophie Ward

Director	Andrew Keates
Set and Costume Designer	Tim McQuillen-Wright
Lighting Designer	Neill Brinkworth
Composer	Matthew Strachan
Sound Designer	Sarah Weltman
Company Stage Manager	Louise Brown
Casting Director	Harry Blumenau
Assistant Designer	Marieke Bernard Berkel
Costume Supervisor	Ugnė Dainiūtė
Videographer	Sara Hutchinson
Graphic Designer	Chris Clegg
Original TV Logo & Merchandise Designer	Clayton Hickman
Production Photographer	Scott Rylander
Public Relations	Chloé Nelkin Consulting
Producer	Rigmarole Productions
General Manager	Rigmarole Productions
Associate Producer	Arion Productions
Associate Producer	JWC Productions
Associate Producer	M Green Productions
Set Construction	MWS Productions Ltd

'See how she leans her cheek upon her hand.
O, that I were a glove upon that hand
That I might touch that cheek!'

Romeo and Juliet,
William Shakespeare

'It won't be easy. It won't be easy without you.'

Theme from *Star Cops* (BBC2, 1987)

Characters

MARIANNE, *early sixties* / RAGANA
OLI, *twenty-one* / VOL
KATE, *late fifties* / PRESIDENT OF EARTH
BOB FRASER, *sixties* / VYKAR
SUZANNE, *mid-fifties* / JAYLIN
KOSLEY, *voice only*

The action takes place over the course of 2016.

Note on the Text

Where there is a line break within a character's dialogue:

MARIANNE. Hmm. You weren't in the bar afterwards.

That's who you remind me of!

it implies a beat or change of thought.

A dash indicates an interruption:

OLI. And I went and saw that, and I'd sent a –

MARIANNE. What was she in?

which can be a self-interruption:

MARIANNE. It was a – European director. They like to experiment.

An ellipsis indicates a trailing-off:

then when I ran into you and, um… And, um…

Also:

Act One: Scenes Two, Four and Seven, and Act Two: Scene Three and the latter half of Scene Four are excerpts from episodes of the fondly remembered, entirely fictitious, telefantasy drama series *Dark Sublime* (ITV, 1979–81). Like similar shows of the era, they should be played full-blooded and sincerely. Though answering to many descriptions, they are not spoofs.

This text went to press before the end of rehearsals and so may differ slightly from the play as performed.

ACT ONE

Scene One

The ident music of Thames Television.

A radiophonic throb establishes, then fades away.

MARIANNE*'s living room. Books, clutter.*

The front door and the main living space are separated only by a small open-plan lobby area; the front door effectively opens into the main space. A door leads from the living space to a kitchen; another one off towards bedroom, bathroom.

The letter box snaps open. A mouth visible.

KATE. I'm going home in a minute!

MARIANNE (*off*). What?

KATE. I'm off!

> MARIANNE *enters, wiping her hands on a tea towel. Perplexed, she looks to the ceiling as though the voice might be coming from above.*

> (*Wearily.*) Behind you.

> MARIANNE *realises there is someone at the front door. She opens it.* KATE *is on her knees.*

MARIANNE. What are you doing?

KATE. What are *you* doing? I've been on the doorstep for ten minutes!

> KATE *moves through and sits on the sofa. She's come from work and is carrying a bottle of wine.*

> Your neighbour must think I'm having a religious experience.

MARIANNE. And are you?

KATE. If you mean 'am I hoping that there's something meaningful at the end of all this suffering' then, yes. A large one.

She hands MARIANNE *the bottle.*

MARIANNE. I've been in the kitchen. I can't hear the bell if I've got Tony Blackburn at full whack.

KATE. 'Another candid glimpse of the home life of one of Britain's top actresses.'

MARIANNE. Well, it was this or the BAFTAs and my Alexander McQueen's in cold soak to try and get that piccalilli out.

KATE. Did you say you were getting a drink?

MARIANNE. Ah, I've always been good at picking up cues. (*Re: wine.*) This?

KATE. Start with a gin and tonic, maybe?

MARIANNE. Gin and tonic. We can do that.

She heads into the kitchen.

You've got a key.

KATE *slips her shoes off, settles back. This back-and-forth is a hallmark of the two women's relationship*

Her phone beeps. She takes it from her bag, looks at it, rummages in her bag, takes out a glasses case, takes the glasses and puts them on, looks again at the phone. She smiles and taps out a reply.

MARIANNE *enters with the drinks. She notices the phone.*

KATE *puts the phone away, then her glasses.* MARIANNE *passes her a drink.*

KATE. I've been dreaming of this all day.

MARIANNE. I say, you've got a key.

KATE. I don't carry it with me. I don't live here.

MARIANNE. Kate – how old are we? You don't have to wait to be invited in.

KATE (*re: the gin and tonic*). Ooh, that's lovely. So we're talking then?

MARIANNE.... We appear to be.

KATE. You know what I mean.

MARIANNE *gets up and crosses to a shelf. She takes down an envelope and hands it to* KATE.

MARIANNE. Read that.

KATE *takes the letter but doesn't open it.*

I notice you said 'top actress' and it's appreciated.

KATE. What did you run away for?

MARIANNE. When?

KATE (*with exaggerated patience*). Saturday.

MARIANNE. Oh! Do you mean you and...

KATE. Suzanne.

MARIANNE. Suzanne. That's right. How is she?

KATE. She's very well.

MARIANNE. Oh, good.

KATE. So...?

MARIANNE. What?

KATE *looks at her.*

I'd left the, um – I'd unplugged the freezer, that's the thing.

KATE *is happy to wait.*

I'd got the fan heater on, for that damp patch – by the swing bin, you know, in the corner? And the kettle was on the go, and I was giving my phone a bit of a bump, and I fancied a crumpet, just before I nipped out, so I had to rejig some of the plugs – and I knew I shouldn't have done it, but it totally slipped my mind, and then when I ran into you and, um… And, um…

KATE *pointedly doesn't help*.

On the street, it suddenly popped back into my head, and I thought – '!' – cos you're not meant to refreeze stuff once it's thawed out, are you?

They didn't factor in the proliferation of electrical appliances when they built these flats.

I wasn't being – Wasn't intending to – Do tell…

KATE. Suz/anne.

MARIANNE. Suzanne. From me.

Pause.

KATE. Mm.

MARIANNE. It was nice to meet her.

KATE. 'Meet' her?!

MARIANNE. She seems lovely.

KATE. She is. Uncomplicated.

MARIANNE. How's work? You haven't read that letter!

KATE. Long day. My Fiesta was clamped over lunch.

MARIANNE. I could never work in an office.

MARIANNE *heads towards the kitchen*.

New shoes?

KATE. These? You've seen these before.

MARIANNE (*off*). They're nice. Suit you.

KATE. Meetings all morning. I always wear a closed-toe if I'm sharing a lift with Outdoor Events.

KATE *has taken the letter from the envelope and started to read.*

MARIANNE (*off*). I saw Liz on Tuesday.

KATE. Oh yes?

MARIANNE (*off*). Nipped round for half an hour. Do my bit. Took her a packet of oat cakes and a *Big Issue*.

KATE. Like the last days of Rome.

MARIANNE (*off*). What d'you say?

KATE. I said that's nice.

MARIANNE *comes back in with a bowl of crisps.*

MARIANNE. She's lost a lot of confidence since the accident.

KATE. Marianne. A toddler bumped into her on his scooter. Hardly *Police Camera Action!*

MARIANNE. Well, that's not very sympathetic.

KATE. Oh god, the arts! If someone looks at you askance you get the vapours! Go into Housing Benefit and answer the phones for an hour. That'll open your eyes.

MARIANNE. She hasn't worked for six months!

KATE. Well, it's not cos of that, is it? That's –

MARIANNE. What?

KATE. Nothing.

MARIANNE. What?

KATE. Well. We both saw the last thing she was in, didn't we?

MARIANNE. It *has* been a long day!

KATE. Is that unfair?

MARIANNE. It was a – European director. They like to experiment.

KATE. Fifty-five pounds to sit on a bench and watch an oversized puppet give birth to a potato.

MARIANNE. It's awful when you know it's not working.

KATE. It's not how *I* remembered *Gypsy*.

MARIANNE. And you always do. You tell yourself it is or you couldn't get up in the morning, but...

She nods at the letter.

What do you think?

KATE. What? Another nutter?

MARIANNE. Oh. I thought it was rather nice.

KATE. It's been a while since you've had one of these.

MARIANNE. I thought he had a nice turn of phrase.

KATE. He can't spell 'charisma'.

MARIANNE. He sounds like a nice lad. I wish I hadn't shown it to you now.

KATE. Don't reply.

MARIANNE. I won't.

KATE. Don't.

MARIANNE. I won't!

I mean, I'll send him a note.

KATE *gives her a look.* MARIANNE *offers the bowl.*

Frazzle?

KATE. I know what you're like with a bit of flattery.

MARIANNE. Not much danger of that round these parts.

KATE. I'm cross with you still.

MARIANNE. Why?

KATE. You know why. You're an idiot sometimes.

MARIANNE. Charming. Would you like to be my agent?

KATE. *Are* you working?

MARIANNE. Um. Next week. Wednesday through Friday.

KATE. Another workshop?

MARIANNE. Vets, this time I think. Tempted to go dressed as a parakeet. See if that keeps us going till they break out the Bourbons.

KATE. Didn't we do all that in the mid-eighties? One of Val's New Years? I remember a lot of feathers.

MARIANNE. Love a costume!

KATE. I've got a photo of you and Darren outside Londis. He's got three bottles of Taboo and you're doing the last reel of *The Scarlet Empress*.

MARIANNE. I was giving my Ophelia!

KATE. You certainly were by the end of the night. To anyone who got within striking distance of the pantry. Don't you remember? I had to plonk you in Val's 2CV.

MARIANNE. 'A prophet is not without honour, but in his own country, and among his own kin, and in his own house.'

KATE. If you'd been in your *own* house there'd have been less of a problem.

MARIANNE. I'd forgotten you'd locked me in a car.

KATE. I didn't lock it! You couldn't work the handle!

MARIANNE. Hmm. Doors have always been a problem. That's why I've never done much provincial touring.

KATE. Three days is good. Must be a lot of vets.

MARIANNE. Oh, I don't know. I haven't read the bumph yet.

Come on, then. What's the story?

KATE. What?

MARIANNE. You know.

'Suzanne'.

KATE. What do you want to know?

MARIANNE. She was at Jill's party, I assume?

KATE. Yes.

MARIANNE. And?

KATE. Well… She was at the party. She's a friend of Paula's –

MARIANNE. Paula has a friend? Rather petit bourgeois.

KATE. And we just got chatting.

Pause.

MARIANNE. God, this is like a mid-week matinee. *And?*

KATE. We had a nice… chat. She works for Barclays.
Paraglides.

MARIANNE. They've branched out.

KATE. Then, you know – the ebb and flow. Duncan got out his
ukulele and…

MARIANNE. Christ.

KATE. I nipped out for a fag. And… She came and asked if
I wanted a drink. And I said yes, so she got us both a drink.
And then we went down to look at Sarah's late-blooming
peonies. Do you really want to hear this?

MARIANNE. We're friends, aren't we?

KATE. We weren't talking about anything consequential. I can't
even remember what we *were* talking about now. The high-
speed rail link or something. Leonard Cohen. Anyway, we
thought we ought to go back inside and we turned to go…
and – I don't know why, I – I don't know why. I kissed her.

MARIANNE. *Did* you?!

KATE. I don't know why I did. I just…

MARIANNE. I expect you wanted to.

KATE. I know, but I'm not sixteen, for god's sake! I haven't
kissed anyone spontaneously since the '97 election!

Pause.

MARIANNE. Well. Perhaps the thought of rapid travel to Birmingham does it for you.

KATE. I've been cutting down on starch recently and I wonder if I was a bit light-headed.

MARIANNE. You've got to stop buying that magazine.

KATE. So.

MARIANNE. How old is she?

KATE. I don't know. Why?

MARIANNE. I'm just thinking of revamping my moisturiser, that's all.

KATE. Nothing wrong with meeting someone new.

MARIANNE. Not at all.

Pause.

Barclays.

KATE. I'm not getting ahead of myself. It's just… It's nice.

MARIANNE. I'm pleased for you.

They wanted me to paraglide on *Pebble Mill* once. I remember some to-do about it. Barry Sheen went up instead and I stayed inside with Trevor Eve and Lulu.

KATE. I mean, it's early days. It might lead to nothing.

MARIANNE. It's led quite far already, from what I gather.

KATE. Well. Let's see.

It hangs in the air.

MARIANNE (*sings with gusto*). 'Come into the garden, Maud! For the black bat night has flo– '

KATE. I didn't mean for that to kill the conversation so conclusively.

MARIANNE. Oh.

It's a bit difficult to top. The most excitement I've had recently is renewing my contents insurance.

KATE. You should have come.

MARIANNE. Well, I might have done if I thought I'd be deflowered in the garden.

KATE. It's not like you weren't invited. Jackie and Iona – they were both asking after you.

MARIANNE. I'm trying to remember the last time I was taken advantage of. I think it was when I was renewing my contents insurance.

KATE. When's dinner?

MARIANNE. All right, I'm just going.

KATE. I had one of those tubs from Pret for lunch. I'm absolutely ravenous.

MARIANNE. It's going to be half an hour.

KATE. I might just nip out quickly.

She indicates 'cigarettes'.

MARIANNE. You'll be on your own. There's no Eve waiting to tempt you out there.

KATE. I'd like you to meet her. Properly, I mean. You'd like her.

MARIANNE. I'm sure.

KATE. Anyway, I wasn't taken advantage of. I was complicit. I was the instigator!

MARIANNE. Have you gone back on the HRT?

KATE. What are we having?

MARIANNE. I kept a few patches back for when I need to get through *Question Time*.

KATE. What are we having?

MARIANNE. Stew.

KATE. Oh, lovely. No one does a stew like you.

MARIANNE *weighs up the full import of that.*

MARIANNE. No.

Scene Two

Blue darkness.

VYKAR *stands alert, poised. He is in his civvies – the uneasy fusion of thirtieth and seventeenth centuries: knee-high boots, buckles, leatherette.*

VYKAR. Show me the schematics.

Green light plays across his face.

Close in. There. Sector six-two-five. Scan.

An electronic beeping. Then the voice of the computer, KOSLEY. It has a refined, some might say prissy, Edinburgh accent.

KOSLEY (*voice-over*). Scanning.

VYKAR. Well?

KOSLEY (*voice-over*). There is a slight trace.

VYKAR. Boost the output.

KOSLEY (*voice-over*). Boosting.

VYKAR. There. Gamma quadrant. Enhance.

KOSLEY (*voice-over*). Enhancing.

VYKAR. Can't you get in any closer than this?

KOSLEY (*voice-over*). I am at peak capacity, Commander!

VYKAR. Come on, you wretched tin box! Come *on*!

KOSLEY (*voice-over*). I'm doing the best I can.

VYKAR. The gods preserve us – !

KOSLEY (*voice-over*). I am at the extent of my range. I can use more power but it will necessitate deactivating the shields –

VYKAR. Do it!

KOSLEY (*voice-over*). – which will, you understand, leave us vulnerable, Commander.

VYKAR. Do it, you – (*Catches himself.*) Just do it.

KOSLEY (*voice-over*). As you insist. Shields deactivating.

The light intensifies. Beeping grows more rapid.

VYKAR. That's it! I was right! We've found her!

Scene Three

MARIANNE*'s flat.* OLI, *twenty-one, and Top Man-trendy is sitting on the sofa.*

He's slightly ill-at-ease – on the edge of the sofa, making sure he's just-so – looking round, taking it all in. He gives his upper arm a rub.

MARIANNE (*from the kitchen*). So, what is it you say you do…?

OLI. Me? I work at Waterstones.

MARIANNE (*off*). No, no, the…

OLI. Oh, the website. Yeah. So, I've been into *Dark Sublime* for, like, ever. But there's hardly anything out there about it – which seems really weird. You think everything's on the internet. But there's only, like, the title sequence and the Shreddies advert on YouTube. Nothing – proper. So I thought 'If no one else is doing anything, why don't I?'

MARIANNE (*off*). Did you?

OLI. And I thought, if I'm doing this I need good-quality content. I mean, there's, like, a limit to the stuff I can get my hands on but I'm, like, really good at talking to people – people say that – so I thought why don't I go out and find people who were in it and talk to them?

MARIANNE (*off*). Do they?

OLI. And then I was at work one day and we were, like, putting out some books, the new Jamie Oliver, so it was, like, September, and this man asked me a question, and I turned

round, you know, to answer him – and it was Maurice Bree!
(*Pronounces it with a long second syllable – 'Maur-eece'.*)
I couldn't believe it! Professor Feldman! Literally, standing
in front of me! I'd never met anyone famous before! I mean,
when I was in Year 7, Charlie from Busted came to our
school cos a girl in Year 9 needed a bone marrow transplant
and I had to – but I mean that doesn't count. So I took him
up to True Crime, and then I thought – this is, like, fate!
Like, it's meant to be! So I took a deep breath and I asked
him if he'd let me interview him. And he didn't quite know
what I meant but he said we should go for a drink / to talk
about it and –

MARIANNE *comes in from the kitchen carrying an old-
fashioned plastic sweet jar.*

MARIANNE. I bet he did.

OLI. And so I, like, went to his place – that was awesome – and
we recorded an interview. My first one!

MARIANNE. How old are you, Oli?

OLI. Twenty-one. Twenty then. My birthday's in November.

MARIANNE. Almost too old for him.

OLI. Oh, no, I –

He was nice.

MARIANNE. Well, I haven't seen Maurice in years.
(*Pronounces it 'Morris' and thereafter so does* OLI.) Snake?

She offers him the sweet jar. OLI *takes a fizzy snake.*

OLI. It was *amazing*, talking to him. So I thought – this is it!
So I started looking then, to see who else I could, like, get.
So, er, I found out that Harriet Monaghan was at the Globe.
The, err, Shakespeare theatre –

MARIANNE. Yes.

OLI. And I went and saw that, and I'd sent a –

MARIANNE. What was she in?

OLI. Um, *Antony and Cleopatra*? She was a servant.

MARIANNE *nods, delighted.*

She was really nice. And Ken Lomax. He runs a pub in Colchester.

MARIANNE. *Ken?* That sounds foolhardy.

OLI. And Barry Turner did an online questionnaire for me.

MARIANNE *thinks.*

MARIANNE. Pentonville?

OLI. Dartmoor.

MARIANNE. Ah.

OLI. But, I mean, like, obviously the person I most wanted to get was you.

MARIANNE *gestures, all benevolence.* OLI *rubs his arm.*

Sorry, that sounds – I mean – it was just, like – it's actually quite big now. The website. Cos it's the only one. Well, the only proper one. There's a guy in Northampton who runs one, but…

He pulls a face.

I mean, I'm the only one going out and interviewing people. And everyone's asking when I was going to interview *you*. So…

MARIANNE. Everyone?

OLI. There's one guy emails me every Thursday about it. And, like – it was obvious, wasn't it? It wasn't like you could have interviews with everyone else from *Dark Sublime* and not you. And, um… I really wanted to meet you, if possible. I can't believe no one's found you before!

MARIANNE. I'm not lost! I get the odd letter. And if I'm on tour someone always turns up at stage door with an old *TV Times*, or that awful picture of me in that leatherette –

She mimes.

OLI. Oh yes!

MARIANNE. I don't touch those. I'll sign anything else.

OLI. Fair enough.

MARIANNE. It's mainly *Emmerdale* I'm recognised for. *Dark Sublime* was so long ago. God knows what it looks like these days.

OLI. I can't believe it's not out on DVD yet. We're starting a petition.

MARIANNE. No, but do you know what is? This dreadful sitcom I did when I was just starting out –

OLI. *Bird in the Hand*?

MARIANNE. Do you know it? Jesus. I'd managed to block it out but this payment slip dropped through the door the other day and you don't turn your nose up at forty quid, do you? Well, maybe *you* do, I don't know. I mean, who's buying that, for Christ's sake?

She looks at him.

OLI. No, not me.

I mean, I've seen it. Seen clips.

He rubs his arm.

MARIANNE. Be like the viewing public. Leave it at that.

Are you all right?

OLI. Oh, yeah, yeah. Sorry. It's my eczema. It gets a bit – when I'm –

He smiles, not wanting to say 'nervous'.

MARIANNE. Don't scratch it.

OLI. No, I'm not.

MARIANNE. David… Oh… David – Lincoln. He had eczema. I did a *Z-Cars* with him. He used to piss into a bottle and dab that on it. Swore it was the only thing that helped. Which might have been true, but was no good if you were spending a whole day in studio with him.

OLI. I've not tried that.

MARIANNE. I've not been able to touch dandelion and burdock since.

But, Oli – how on earth did you find out about *Dark Sublime*? You weren't *born* when it was on! Or the one time it was repeated! Where's it come from? What can it possibly have to offer you?

OLI. Er – it's good! It's really good! Uh, I mean, it's exciting and there's, like, a really good cast. Great writing and direction. It's just… Yeah.

MARIANNE. You should write for *Time Out*.

OLI. Sorry. I mean, I've always been into telefantasy. Not science-fiction as such but – offbeat, weird stuff. And I kept coming across the name, you know, in articles, but I'd never seen it. And one of my mates on – I'm on an Archive TV forum – he sent me these three DVDs that he'd burnt – I mean, the quality wasn't great, it was all from, like, a fourth-generation VHS copy –

MARIANNE. Do you provide a glossary for this conversation?

OLI. But, you know – to see it finally! Got me through my GCSEs! I'd watch one a night, to make it last. And then, like, did the whole thing in one go at the end. It's so cool.

MARIANNE. Extraordinary.

And people are asking you to interview me?

OLI. Yeah! Course they are! You're Ragana!

MARIANNE. And it'd be a… module?

OLI. Podcast.

MARIANNE. Podcast, yes. Okay, well. It doesn't sound… Shall we have a drink? Let's have a drink. You get fed up of tea.

OLI. Sure. Awesome.

*She moves towards the kitchen but pulls a framed
photograph from a shelf and hands it to him.*

MARIANNE. Look at that. Me, Moira Stuart, and King Juan
Carlos of Spain. That was a night.

OLI. Who are all the –

MARIANNE. Crew of the *Ark Royal*.

She winks, then disappears into the kitchen. OLI *replaces
the picture on the shelf. We hear activity from the kitchen.*
OLI *looks round the room, taking it all in. He peers at
another picture.*

OLI. It smells really nice in here.

MARIANNE *enters with two glasses and an open bottle of
red wine.*

Is that Louise Webber?

MARIANNE. What? That? No. That's – my friend Kate. Louise
Webber?!

She peers at the picture.

Ha!

OLI. Is she an actress?

MARIANNE. Kate? You must be joking!

No.

OLI. She looks amazing.

MARIANNE. We all dressed like that, back then. Even if you
worked for the local authority. Especially! There you go.

She hands him a glass of wine.

OLI. Thanks.

MARIANNE. Christ, the idea of having a picture of Louise
Webber on display. Even her agent wouldn't commit to that.

(*Re: wine*.) Now, *that's* good-quality content.

Shall we start then?

OLI. Oh, sure. Yes.

OLI *takes his phone from his pocket along with a small portable USB microphone. He plugs the mic into the phone.*

MARIANNE. That's very neat.

OLI. Oh, yeah.

MARIANNE. We had those controls for opening the doors on the show. Do you know the ones I mean? They were the size of house bricks. Weren't awfully prescient, were we?

OLI *has opened his recording app. Checks it's working.* MARIANNE *is a dab hand at covering this 'dead time', pre-interview.*

Rocks – now, they were a different matter. We used to enjoy rocks. Three years at RADA, winner of the William Poel Memorial Award for Verse Speaking, and here I am, trying to invest this lump of polystyrene with the elusive property of *weight*. No help from Stanislavski on *that* score.

Ready?

OLI *takes a folded sheet of A4 from his pocket.*

OLI. Er, yeah.

MARIANNE. I thought DVDs were obsolete?

OLI. Um –

MARIANNE. Isn't it all –

She waves airily above her head.

OLI….

MARIANNE. That's what it said in the *Sunday Times*.

OLI. Streamed, you mean? Like Netflix?

MARIANNE. Y-e-s…?

OLI. Yeah, I suppose. But not for, like, this kind of stuff. Archive. Cult. DVD's the only way to get it. Netflix aren't gonna touch it.

MARIANNE (*oddly disappointed*). Oh.

She indicates – 'Shall we?'

OLI. Right. Um. How did you get the part of Ragana?

MARIANNE. Good. Er. We were at the Theatre Royal. I got a call from my agent saying Terry – Terence Kelly – wondered if I'd come in for a new show he was getting together over at Thames. I'd worked with him before on a season of Ibsen plays that LWT had done earlier in the year, so we were old friends. He said he'd thought of me when developing this character, Ragana. She was this... ice queen, stuck in this other dimension, looking for this... crystal, which held the secret of, the meaning of, life. Or her life. Or something.

OLI. A Shadow Ruby. She needed it to become whole.

MARIANNE. Shadow Ruby, that's right. 'Shadow Ruby'! And, so you think, 'Well!'

I mean, I was just starting to become typecast in light comedy at this point – it was heading that way – so I was looking for something... a bit different. She was going to be... cold. Callous. Bit of a bitch. Terry had this joke that he thought I'd be perfect after seeing me order a haddock mousse in the BBC canteen, but... that was just a line he liked to trot out.

Though they could be very stingy, you know, those girls.

Anyway. I thought there was interesting scope there for... with the way my character would interact with Bob and Wendy. Not that they were cast at that stage. Bob was my suggestion; I knew he'd be just right for... um –

OLI. Vykar.

MARIANNE. That's it. So I went in and read for Terry and Brian Scarborough and they offered it me there and then.

OLI. Did you have any say in the development of the character?

MARIANNE. Well, there were times when I would disagree with what had been written – and I'm talking about before it started getting silly, with all the – rampaging lobsters and… hats, and god knows what –

But there wasn't a lot of time in rehearsals to… You just had to get on and do it. Nowadays you're lucky if you *get* a rehearsal, of course – which is very unlike life, if you think about it, which is all fucking rehearsal and no fucking performance.

She notices OLI*'s reaction.*

Oh, sorry. Do you need me to –

OLI. It's okay.

MARIANNE. Wait –

Beat.

Nowadays you're lucky if you *get* a rehearsal, of course – which is very unlike life, if you think about it, which is *all* rehearsal and *no* performance.

OLI *smiles at seeing the craft upfront.* MARIANNE *winks at him, enjoying the admiration.*

Then: the default text-message tone.

Oh, hang on. That's me, isn't it?

She searches and finds her phone.

Now, one moment. Oh, I need my – where are they?

She finds her glasses.

Let's look at this.

She reads the text message.

Oh, I knew she – I *did* tell her!

My friend's gone out tonight. With her – friend. But she can't follow directions. Let me just…

She taps a reply.

OLI. Joel's like that. My friend. He couldn't find his arse without Google Maps.

MARIANNE *looks up. Nods towards the microphone.* OLI *checks his next question.*

Um. Over the course of the series, certainly the first two series in particular, there are a number of episodes that explore wider issues: pollution in 'The Nightmare Dust', the rise of the National Front in 'White Heat', the stranglehold of the trade unions in 'Crisis on Pajarax Five' – I wondered how much of that you were aware of, as actors, when rehearsing and whether it was something you were sorry to see phased out?

MARIANNE. Christ.

We were just trying to fill thirty minutes of television. I don't mean it wasn't good, that we weren't trying to make *good* television, but…

OLI. But the show does, like, focus on big themes. It explores – um. Like, the title's taken from an Auden poem –

MARIANNE. Oh, well, that was Brian, wasn't it? Showing off. Doesn't one of them have lines from a pop song or something?

OLI. Oh, Boney M., yeah.

MARIANNE. Right. So. Hardly high art.

OLI. I just thought, there does seem to be a deliberate emphasis on, um, like, loneliness. Loss.

MARIANNE. Oli! You could say the same about my current account!

There were – themes we explored, I suppose. But it was a fantasy. The idea that we set out to critique the – three-day week or whatever… I think it's easy to read in meanings that aren't there. As in life. Ha!

OLI. But, like – even Joel picked up on the National Front stuff and he's…

MARIANNE. What?

OLI. Well. You have to, like, spell things out sometimes.

MARIANNE. Yes, well… Of course, at the time, a lot of that
stuff was in the air. But I'm not sure *I'd* expect to find
answers to the fundamental questions at teatime on ITV.

Another text message.

What's this?

She peers at the phone.

Oh, she's found it now. The bar.

Well, that was anti-climactic, wasn't it? Still. Nice of her to
check in.

OLI. Joel's just like that. I'm always telling him, like, what
times buses are and stuff. He's useless!

MARIANNE. Mmm?

OLI. My friend. The one I've been introducing the show to.

MARIANNE. You tell him what time buses are?

OLI. Yeah. If he wants to… catch one…

He loves you! He thinks you're awesome!

MARIANNE. Does he?

MARIANNE *is gazing absently at her phone.* OLI *rubs
his arm.*

OLI. When you turn to the camera and say 'I have waited
millennia for you, *worm*. Now your screams will echo
beyond time!'… It's just…!

MARIANNE. Ha!

OLI. I mean, wow!

MARIANNE. Yes, you don't get chance to deliver lines like
that very often. Although I have a go, now and then, mainly
when I'm at the chiropodist.

OLI *laughs.*

Well, I suppose that's that.

She puts the phone down.

'Introducing the show to'…!

She tops up their glasses.

OLI. He is gonna be pretty much rendered speechless when I tell him about this!

MARIANNE. It's – nice to have an impact.

OLI. He is gonna be soooo jealous!

MARIANNE. Well… I don't want to create a rift between you.

OLI. Oh, no! We're, like, best buds!

MARIANNE.…Good.

OLI. But he wouldn't be comfortable here, in this kind of situation. Joel's more… He needs to warm up, you know? He can't go in cold. Whereas I'm comfortable talking to anyone! I'll talk to literally anyone!

MARIANNE. I believe you.

OLI. But I think that's why the friendship works so well.

MARIANNE. I'm sure.

OLI. Are you still friends with Eileen Russell?

MARIANNE. – !

Not since she stole my idea for *Pendleton Park* and got four series and a Portuguese villa out of it, no.

Come on, then. Show me a picture.

OLI. Of…?

MARIANNE. I'm sure you've got one.

OLI. Of Joel?

MARIANNE. No, that awful pub we used to stay at on location!

It worries me that you might actually have that.

OLI. Um –

OLI has picked up his phone and is scrolling through.
He leans back, sharply, not wanting that *photo to be seen.*
MARIANNE, *not versed in sexting, remains oblivious.*

There.

He shows MARIANNE.

MARIANNE. I see. Handsome lad.

OLI. Yeah.

MARIANNE. If I had cheekbones like that I'd be getting driven round the streets every night on a flatbed lorry so everyone could have a look.

OLI. I know.

MARIANNE *looks at him. Smiles.*

MARIANNE. Twenty-one! I'm trying to remember being twenty-one. Though I wasn't much older when we were making *Dark Sublime*. Twenty… Well, no, I was. Twenty-eight. Twenty-eight!

OLI. You look great, though.

MARIANNE. *Then* I did.

OLI. And now.

MARIANNE. You've got a silver tongue!

OLI. You do! And it's so exciting to have a strong female lead. And that was, like, thirty-five years ago!

MARIANNE. Yes, it *was* good on that score, I suppose.

OLI. It was. Progressive. You know – strong female roles. Lots of, like, inclusive casting…

MARIANNE. Ha! Terry got called a lot of things as producer but progressive's a new one!

OLI. It was ahead of its time!

MARIANNE. *You* weren't in the bar afterwards.

That's who you remind me of!

OLI. Who?

MARIANNE. There was a lad with the look of you in the last episode. What was his name?

OLI. In 'Were Stars to Burn'? Someone like me?

MARIANNE. Not the last one, sorry. The one they didn't show. We recorded it last. I can see his face.

OLI. The one they *didn't* show?

MARIANNE. Yes, it was meant to be the final episode. I finally meet up with the – young boy, whatever his name was –

OLI. Vol?

MARIANNE. Vol! 'Vol'!

OLI. You get to see Vol?!

MARIANNE. Well, that was the plan. I forget why it didn't go out now. Was it a strike?

OLI. There's a whole episode that wasn't shown…?

MARIANNE. There was a lot of industrial action around that time. We never got to finish it. I think we missed the final studio session. That's right. We were locked out. It's coming back to me now.

OLI. I didn't know about this!

MARIANNE. Oh, I assumed… But, then, why would you? I found the script for it a few months back, actually.

OLI. Really?!

MARIANNE. I say 'a few months'. It would've been – last Easter, cos I was digging out the sleeping bag.

OLI. Have you still got it?

MARIANNE. You want to stay over?

OLI....

No, I mean, the script!

MARIANNE. Oh. Good.

Um. Pffff. Maybe. Hard to say in amongst all this tut.

OLI *is stretched taut.*

OLI. I'd love to see it.

MARIANNE. Well, I'll keep an eye out. I wouldn't get your hopes up though.

OLI. A whole secret episode!

MARIANNE. Well, not 'secret'. Just not talked about. There's a difference.

OLI. I can't believe it!

MARIANNE. Christ, if discussing things that never got made excites you, we'll have a jamboree!

OLI. Can you remember the plot?

MARIANNE. Oh... Not with *that* amount left in the glass. You need to learn how to drink.

OLI. I'm not really a big wine drinker.

MARIANNE. I can see. Good bottle, that, too. Château de Tesco Metro. Brings the taps up a treat.

OLI. It is nice, though. And it's so kind of you to, like, spare the time for me. It's so amazing being here. You're so fab!

MARIANNE *exhales, modestly, at a loss.*

You are! You're awesome!

MARIANNE *struggles with rebuffing this – then gives up.*

MARIANNE. Oli! Well, get it down you – *(Re: microphone.)* turn that off and then I'm opening some champagne.

OLI. Really?

MARIANNE. Yes. Cos you, young man, are about to get all my best anecdotes – including why, and at whose behest, the set for *Farmhouse Kitchen* had to be chemically sterilised following the 1987 Yorkshire Television Christmas Party.

I feel like getting pissed!

Scene Four

VYKAR *continues to scan the ship's instruments.*

VYKAR. This could be it. I'm not going to let this slip through my fingers. Send an automated communicapsule to the Collective Command Dome. Implant it with my ident-key. And put us into a geo-stationary orbit. Somewhere close.

The sound of mighty engines powering down.

KOSLEY (*voice-over*). We are now in geo-stationary orbit above Zone Two.

VYKAR. Have you set up that energy pulse yet?

KOSLEY (*voice-over*). Commander, I don't think you fully appreciate the complexi–

VYKAR. Do it!

KOSLEY (*voice-over, sigh*). Very well.

Electronic ping!

Energy pulse activated.

VYKAR. Good.

KOSLEY (*voice-over*). Though I really don't see why –

VYKAR. She'll think we're headed in one direction – the alpha quadrant – when in reality I'll be able to sneak up through gamma and surprise her.

KOSLEY (*voice-over*). Ingenious.

VYKAR. Where are the others?

KOSLEY (*voice-over*). The others?

VYKAR. The rest of the team. Where are they?

KOSLEY (*voice-over*). Oh, the *others*. Jaylin and Tarak are reassembling the Hyperdrive Thermo-Shields, Paval and Nyundai are jamming transmissions from the NewsCom satellites, Vol is still trapped in a parallel dimension – and Marec is in his room and says he's not to be disturbed.

VYKAR. By the gods – !

He touches his wrist communicator. Beep!

Marec.

Marec!

MAREC!

KOSLEY (*voice-over*). I've already tried. There is no answer.

VYKAR. What does he *do* in there?

KOSLEY (*voice-over*). I couldn't say, Commander. He has overridden my security camera.

VYKAR *sighs*.

VYKAR. Then I'll go alone. Kosley, I'm going to get suited up. I want you to keep scanning and let me know immediately if anything changes down there. When Jaylin, Tarak, Pavel, or Nyundai finish what they're doing, get them to standby on the transmat controls.

Vol – you will be avenged.

Marec – I'll deal with you later.

This is it. No one's ever got this close before. Don't lose her, Kosley, or I'll tear you apart and sell you for scrap in the junkyards of Blitoris!

He exits.

KOSLEY (*voice-over*). Well, *really* – !

Scene Five

A bar. MARIANNE *and* OLI *have met for a drink.*
MARIANNE *sits at a table.*

OLI *comes to the table carrying a large glass of red wine and
a pint of cider.*

OLI. There you go.

He puts down the drinks and sits.

MARIANNE. Haven't you got lovely cheery underpants?

The cider is at his lips.

I was just thinking that as you went to the bar.

OLI. Oh, er –

He makes an attempt to hitch his trousers up while seated.

MARIANNE. No, no. I know that's how things are nowadays.

I'm not a prude. I once did a naked shoot. For Timotei. Well,
three strips of gaffa tape and a small polythene square, but
that doesn't count for much when you're in front of twenty
hairy technicians in a derelict warehouse north of Antwerp.

Did that wine come out of your trousers?

OLI. Oh. Yeah.

MARIANNE. Go a bit slower tonight, eh?

He smiles, abashed. Gives his arm a small rub.

OLI. I finished George Cook's autobiography last night.

MARIANNE. George Cook's written an autobiography?!

OLI. Yeah.

MARIANNE. What – published?

OLI. There's a small firm that specialises in, like, telefantasy
memoirs and archive research.

MARIANNE. I bet their Christmas party's a hoot.

OLI. He's a councillor now. For UKIP. There's not much about the show. He gets quite cross about, like... pavements.

MARIANNE *nods. Typical!*

Are you still friends with anyone? It feels like there was, like, a good relationship between you all.

MARIANNE. No!

I'm barely in contact with the people I *want* to see! This is the second time *we've* met, you and I. Do you now how unlikely that is? We're practically married!

OLI. I don't want to take up your time, if you've got other people to, like...

MARIANNE. Other people?

OLI. Friends.

MARIANNE. Oh! No. No, no, no.

I don't want to sound condescending, Oli, but when you get older –

OLI. Did you – I don't know if you looked...?

You said you might have that script. The untransmitted episode.

MARIANNE. Oh. Er... No, I didn't. I mean, the chances of it being around are...

OLI. Sure. Just thought I'd...

Pause.

MARIANNE. I had a look at your website.

OLI. Oh, did you?

MARIANNE. Very – comprehensive.

OLI. It's mainly a lot of, like, static text at the moment. Apart from the podcasts. I'm trying to get more images together.

MARIANNE. Your page on Bob's very cheeky.

OLI. Oh – ! It's just… It's not meant to be offensive.

MARIANNE. No, he *did* always do that thing with his hands.

OLI. It's not a criticism. It's just a – funny thing. I'm not, like, taking the –

MARIANNE. Piss? Well, you are, but that's all right.

Oh, it's odd talking about all this again. *Dark Sublime*.
All that.

OLI. It's awesome listening to you!

MARIANNE. You're very good for the soul, Oli! I might make you a full-time member of staff.

OLI *laughs, thrilled*.

I've never had that kind of passion for anything.

I mean, I quite like *Countryfile* but I wouldn't go out of my way.

OLI. I just love it.

MARIANNE. Oh, it's not been the same since John Craven took a back seat.

OLI. No, I mean being a fan. Chatting with other people. Sharing stuff you like – all the brilliant episodes, or laughing at the – enjoying the…

MARIANNE. Crap ones?

OLI. Y-e-a-h! But still *enjoying* them. There's always *something* interesting in every episode. Like the one in the Butlins holiday camp –

MARIANNE. Oh, yes.

OLI. Or the, uh – the one about the Marquis de Sade. I mean, that's, like, mental!

MARIANNE. That's still never been shown in Ulster.

OLI. When… (Huh!)

When I was at school… It wasn't really – great. You know. At all. And I used to come home, and… I'd be in my room.

And it'd be, like, just getting dark. My favourite time. And you could hear people outside, like, in the street. Cars. And I'd put an episode on. And it'd, like – take me away. And you used to come on, in those dresses, those, like, amazing costumes, and you were just… Like, you were… The things you said. The way you spoke. The way you *stood*. It made me… You were so… It was, like – life *can* be different, you know? From the way it… sometimes – is.

Pause.

MARIANNE. So you became a drag queen?

OLI. What? No!

MARIANNE. I'm joking!

Half-joking. I have had *other* letters.

OLI. That was lame. Sorry.

MARIANNE. No, don't be silly. It's… It's interesting.

How's… (*Thinks.*) Joel?

OLI. Oh. Um. Fine. He's, er – playing football tonight.

MARIANNE. You don't play?

OLI. No!

MARIANNE. No.

OLI. I go running sometimes. Not often. But…

He shakes his head.

MARIANNE. Kate does pilates. She keeps asking me if I'll go. Well, she did. But who wants to stand in a Methodist hall surrounded by sweaty bodies while someone yells instructions at you? There was enough of that when I campaigned for Labour in '83.

OLI. Joel's in a five-a-side team. It's funny, really, cos we're, like, so similar in so many ways, but *that*…

He shrugs.

I did go to watch him once, you know. But… boring.

MARIANNE. There are some fringe benefits, though, surely?

He looks at her.

Boys in shorts.

OLI. Oh, yeah. But, no. Fit lads, yeah, but...

He shrugs.

And you can't see that much anyway. You know, you look at old footage from, like, the eighties and the shorts are amazing. Proper shorts!

MARIANNE. You don't watch old football matches too?

OLI. No! God! I just mean, if you see clips.

Can't think of anything worse.

MARIANNE. No.

They stare into the abyss.

OLI. What *is* pilates?

MARIANNE. Err...

OLI. Is it like Zumba?

MARIANNE. I don't know.

Pause.

OLI. You did aerobics, though, on *TV-am*, didn't you?

MARIANNE. Jesus, what a thing to pull out of the ether! Did I?

OLI. It's on YouTube.

MARIANNE. Is it?! Christ.

OLI. It's quite funny. You don't look like you really want to be there.

MARIANNE. I didn't! That was when I went into *Emmerdale*. They were hawking me round everywhere. 'You get up at five o'clock and squeeze yourself into stretch lycra if it's that important!' I said: 'Not me they want to see, toots!' And now, what? It's all over the internet?

OLI. Well, you have to look for it.

She looks at him.

MARIANNE. You don't *have* to. Is there anything that isn't immediately retrievable nowadays? Other than what we say when we're drunk?

OLI. A girl at school uploaded seven pics of Lewis Bradley naked when they split.

Beat.

MARIANNE. Is that iambic pentameter?

OLI. He didn't seem that bothered. Thick as shit.

She runs it through her head – delighted to discover it is.

Beautiful, though.

We watched 'Children of Kronos' last night. Joel and me.

MARIANNE. Which one's that?

OLI. Series two, episode four. Where you capture Mowax in the time web.

Nothing.

All about immortality and the necessity of death.

Nope.

The exteriors were filmed at the lingerie factory in Bristol.

MARIANNE. Oh yes.

OLI. 'Have you heard of Prometheus, boy? An old story from Earth. A myth. But I gift you reality. Bathe me in your screams!'

MARIANNE. We had fun on that one.

OLI. We're always saying that to each other.

MARIANNE. We all got given free knickers at the end. All the women. Until the boys complained that they should be given some. 'For their girlfriends.'

OLI. 'Bathe me in your screams!'

MARIANNE. Kate came out for that one, now I think about it. She wanted to see what I did. *That* dates it.

OLI. It really works, being on location, rather than studio.

MARIANNE. She was bored senseless. I did warn her.

OLI. God, I'm jealous! I'd love to have been there!

MARIANNE. It pains me to say it, Oli, but not everyone's as fascinated by me as you.

OLI. Can't really ask Joel to come and watch me at work. Not really the same thing.

MARIANNE. No.

But you must do other things. Go and see a film. Take him to dinner!

OLI. Yes. Yes.

MARIANNE. Go to a – gig. I don't know. You don't need advice from an old fart like me! Woo him! We all want to be wooed.

OLI. Yes.

MARIANNE. *Have* you asked him?

OLI. No. Not – I…

MARIANNE. Ask him. You won't know till you do, will you?

OLI. No. No, I – Yeah.

Sorry. Bit embarrassed.

MARIANNE. Don't be. Look at you! Beautiful boy.

OLI *exhales a shy laugh*.

OLI. No. Okay.

It's just weird, sitting here. Talking to – *you*. About Joel.

MARIANNE. I like you, kid.

OLI. !

    Well. I like *you*.

MARIANNE. Good!

    Now, you'd better tell me about this convention.

Scene Six

MARIANNE*'s flat – three weeks later.*

KATE *is sitting on the sofa.* MARIANNE *is in the kitchen.*

KATE. Where?

MARIANNE (*off*). Walsall.

KATE. *Where?*

MARIANNE (*off*). Walsall!

KATE. 'Walsall'!

    Are you going?

MARIANNE (*off*). I don't know. Why not?

    She enters with a bottle of champagne and two glasses.

    Everything's got to be somewhere. There you go.

KATE. Oh, no, I'm not drinking tonight.

MARIANNE. What do you mean you're not drinking?

KATE. We got into a second bottle last night.

MARIANNE. Who did?

KATE. Me and Suzanne.

MARIANNE. Oh, you and Suzanne.

KATE. Yes.

MARIANNE. I've opened it now.

KATE. Why've you got Prosecco?

MARIANNE. Champagne!

KATE. Champagne then.

MARIANNE. 'Prosecco'! I thought it would be a nice thing to do.

KATE. Why?

MARIANNE. I haven't seen you in a month.

KATE. Three weeks.

MARIANNE. I'm just saying it's nice to see you. There was a bottle in the fridge. I didn't go out specially.

I'll be dead one day!

KATE. We'll all be dead one day.

MARIANNE. Maybe tomorrow. Maybe tomorrow morning I'll be run over by a bus, by the 159 – which is entirely poss–

KATE. I'm drinking.

They both drink. Pause.

MARIANNE. Well, this is nice.

KATE. Is anyone else going?

MARIANNE. Wendy. Brian. Maurice Bree – he was always a dead cert. Dougie Graham. And some of the effects boys, I think.

KATE. And will there actually be people there?

MARIANNE. They've sold all the tickets, apparently.

KATE. How many's that?

MARIANNE. Five hundred.

KATE. *Five hundred?!*

MARIANNE. Apparently so.

KATE. Five hundred people have paid to spend the weekend in Walsall listening to you talk about a job you did thirty-five years ago?!

MARIANNE. I'm very entertaining!

KATE. You certainly are right now. So you've *got* to go, then. If you've been advertised.

MARIANNE. 'Subject to work commitments.'

Pause.

KATE. So you've got to go, then.

MARIANNE. Awful.

KATE. Are they paying you?

MARIANNE. Accommodation and travel.

KATE *gives* MARIANNE *a look.*

It's for Cystic Fibrosis!

KATE. What is?

MARIANNE. Any profit! It's a charity thing.

KATE. You can say that again.

And this boy's running it?

MARIANNE. He's got some involvement but it's not all him.

He's nice!

KATE. I was surprised that you invited him here, I admit. But I'm more surprised that you've been for a drink with him.

MARIANNE. What's wrong with going for a drink? I like going for a drink. Anyway, he was / interviewing me.

KATE. I think it's odd. Don't reply, I said!

MARIANNE. He's a nice lad, Kate. He's got a bit of… vim about him. He makes me laugh. That's why, I suppose. I like to laugh.

KATE. You can't be friends with a fan.

MARIANNE. I'm not his friend!

KATE. Does he know that? He's twenty-one.

MARIANNE. Oh, *now* age is problematic!

KATE. What's that supposed to mean?

MARIANNE. Nothing.

KATE. You worry me when you get like this.

MARIANNE. What does *that* mean?

KATE. You know what I mean. You get carried away with
    things. I don't want you to be…

MARIANNE. Look, they're interested in me. They want to
    know what… we did in rehearsals and what jokes we played
    on location, and *they* want to tell *me* how marvellous I am!
    That's all. I like being told I'm marvellous. I *am* marvellous!
    I mean, it'd be nice if other people said it now and again…

KATE. Remember that book group?

MARIANNE. Oh, don't start with that.

KATE. Lovely people. Interesting conversation. All that.

MARIANNE. Y-e-s.

KATE. Four weeks that lasted.

MARIANNE. That's not fair. Cults don't reveal themselves.
    They lure you in.

KATE. I'm only saying. You went at that full pelt. All that stuff
    I had to print out for you –

MARIANNE. I'm not going at anything! I'm just – being
    sociable! Getting out of the… pissing house! Like you said.

    Pause.

KATE. I remember going at the draining board with Vim when
    we moved into our first place, me and Mike. That first night.
    We had fish and chips cos the gas wasn't on and we sat and ate
    them with our backs to the partition wall, and everything was

orange from the street lamp outside. I haven't thought about that in years. We had sex that night on a mattress. No bed, cos his brother was bringing it round the next day in his van – that, and a second-hand twin-tub that his dad had got from an ad in the free paper. And I got up at two o'clock that morning and locked myself in the bathroom and cried and cried.

I bet you can't get Vim any more.

MARIANNE *has paused to frame the next question exactly right.* KATE *sees this.*

We're not 'talking'. That was just a – thing. Don't really know why I said it. Making odd connections. Like you!

MARIANNE. Jesus! I hadn't said anything!

KATE. No, but. How were the vets? Do they know how to deal with emotion now?

MARIANNE. They're fine. Very stable.

Pause.

I'm 'awesome', apparently.

KATE. We don't read reviews, remember?

MARIANNE. A compliment isn't a review.

KATE. That's what I've been saying for the past thirty-odd years!

MARIANNE *takes out a small paper bag of sweets.*

MARIANNE. Sour lemon?

KATE *ignores her.* MARIANNE *puts them away.*

So, how about it?

KATE. What?

MARIANNE. You going to come?

KATE. Am *I* going to come?

MARIANNE. Yes.

KATE. Why would *I* want to go?

MARIANNE. Keep me company.

KATE. You'll have company! There's all the others going.

MARIANNE. Oh, *hardly*. Wendy and Brian'll be simpering round the affair they were too spineless to have in 1980, Maurice Bree'll be offering late-night 'acting lessons' to any wide-eyed lad under twenty, and Dougie Graham'll be cross-legged in a corner, meditating. Or, worse, trying to get all of us to meditate *with* him. We haven't been away together in ages. We could have fun.

KATE. In Walsall?

MARIANNE. We're not under lock and key. I'm only on the Saturday afternoon, and part of the evening. And Sunday from eleven till two. We can go out.

KATE. In Walsall?

MARIANNE. Birmingham's down the road.

KATE. Be still, my beating heart.

MARIANNE....

KATE. I don't really want to sit in a Premier Inn waiting for you to – finish – whatever it is that you're – going to be doing.

MARIANNE. But that's not a 'no'...

KATE. And I might want to do something with Suzanne that weekend.

MARIANNE. I haven't said what weekend it is.

KATE. It doesn't matter.

MARIANNE. Oh. Right.

> KATE *waggles her empty glass.*

I thought you weren't drinking?

KATE. You've opened the bottle now. But just this.

> MARIANNE *refills their glasses.*

What jokes *did* you play on location?

MARIANNE *thinks*.

MARIANNE. I told Brian Scarborough his script was demeaning whippet shit and threw it down a slag heap. Does that count?

KATE. Was it a joke?

MARIANNE. His idea of feminism was.

KATE. Are you going to say that at this event?

MARIANNE. I'll see how the mood takes me.

KATE. He pulled it together quickly, this boy. How long's he been planning it?

MARIANNE. I don't know. I suppose, if you put your mind to something... I replaced all my cushion covers one weekend.

KATE. Yes, that's exactly the same thing.

MARIANNE. I think you'd enjoy it.

KATE. Look, once you're there you'll be wrapped up in it all. They'll be asking you questions and taking photos and asking you to sign things. I've seen it all before.

MARIANNE. I've never done one of these before!

KATE. I've seen you when someone's recognised you. That time we went to Whitby.

MARIANNE. That was nothing! What was that?

KATE. Oh, come off it! You *loved* it! Giving autographs, posing for photos.

MARIANNE. What did you want me to do? Ignore them?

KATE. It was a *funeral*!

MARIANNE. The service had finished! They were just hanging around! There was no coffin!

KATE. Scribbling on Orders of Service. I was *mortified*.

MARIANNE. It's part of the job –

KATE. How these people recall who they've seen on television fifteen years previously is beyond me. It's all I can do to remember if I'm running low on milk before I've gone past Sainsbury's.

MARIANNE. Some people appreciate the contribution I've made to their lives –

KATE. Don't give me that. I'm just saying, you'll be in your element. Five hundred – *five hundred!* – people gazing at you adoringly? Seventh heaven. You won't want me there.

MARIANNE. I *do* want you there.

KATE. Don't be silly.

MARIANNE. It's not silly.

KATE. Well.

Pause.

I was thinking of making something to eat one evening. So you can meet properly. Maybe ask Liz, too.

MARIANNE. Meet who?

KATE. You don't have to come.

MARIANNE. That'd be a nice thing to do. I'd like that.

KATE. Okay. Well. I haven't decided yet. I was just mentioning it.

MARIANNE. It'd be nice to meet her properly.

KATE *looks at her.*

KATE. These people are going to ask you questions about your acting, are they?

Pause.

MARIANNE. Come over on Friday.

KATE. For what?

MARIANNE. For a drink. Come on Friday for a drink. I've nothing on.

KATE. Suzanne's coming to mine.

MARIANNE. Well – bring her here.

KATE. I'm going to try that sea bass.

MARIANNE. You can do that any – That sea bass you did for me?

KATE. Yes.

MARIANNE. Oh.

KATE. I want to give it another go. Now I know what I'm doing.

MARIANNE. You can do that any time. Come here.

KATE. Um...

MARIANNE. If you want.

KATE. Let me see. Let me ask her.

MARIANNE. She won't object, will she?

KATE. No, it's just – We'd planned something else. So let me run it by her.

MARIANNE. She'll be able to get the time off college, won't she? THAT WAS A JOKE!

KATE *gives her a look*.

I was just joking! Just having a laugh!

KATE (*dry as the Gobi*). Hm. Singular.

MARIANNE. We'll have a nice time.

KATE. Will we.

MARIANNE. Yes.

KATE. Okay.

MARIANNE. Good.

That'll be nice.

I'll look forward to that.

Scene Seven

VYKAR *enters, laser pistol drawn. A beep as he touches his wrist communicator.*

VYKAR. Kosley, I'm down. If your calculations are correct, I've entered the gamma quadrant. I'm going to keep this channel open. You need to be ready to take me up the moment I give the word.

KOSLEY (*voice-over*). But of course.

VYKAR. Are the others on the bridge yet?

KOSLEY (*voice-over*). They are still about their business, Commander. Apart from Marec who is now in the hygiene chamber. And Vol, who is still trapped in a parallel –

VYKAR. Yes, yes! Well. Make sure they keep sending out the signal. And ask Jaylin to transmat down and join me. It's working. Ragana's close. I can feel it.

KOSLEY (*voice-over*). I certainly will. Commander?

VYKAR. What is it?

Pause.

Kosley?

KOSLEY (*voice-over*). Be careful.

VYKAR *considers. Nods. Exits.*

Scene Eight

MARIANNE*'s flat. Friday evening.*

OLI *is dressed smartly. He sits, rapt. A bottle of champagne sits open, glasses poured.*

MARIANNE (*off*). I haven't really got a favourite story. I didn't watch them, you see. You'll find very few actors that enjoy watching themselves. Actors are a very insecure lot, let me tell you. Maybe that's not a surprise to you. They've a lot to be insecure about, you might think. And, in the case of a rather well-known chap who's currently getting away with murder in the Lyttleton each evening and twice at weekends, you'd be right.

She enters from the kitchen, carrying a small bowl. Though in the familiar confines of her flat, she might as well be onstage as she holds court for OLI, *who is lapping up this exclusive audience.*

There was one set in a lighthouse, wasn't there? That was very good. Very droll. That had – was that the one with Pat Bradwell? Was it?

OLI. Yes. 'The Sirens of Blood Rock'.

MARIANNE. He was a hoot, old Paddy. I had this enormous ruff on my right shoulder in that one, like someone had run into me and the airbag had gone off. Incredible thing – I kept listing to the right like a cheap ferry. And he'd made some crack, just before we started – that was something he liked to do – so I positioned myself so it was masking him. Every shot. You could see the boys on the cameras trying to adjust to get him in. Only a bit of fun. He could hold his own, Paddy. And sometimes did, if it was a tight two-shot. I think that's what got him the elbow from *Juliet Bravo*. Was it Ted Bailey who wrote that?

OLI. Yes.

MARIANNE. He did quite a few for us. They were the ones you didn't want to hurl across the room. He could spin a good line,

Ted. Of course, he'd been an ambulance driver for twenty years. He'd seen life. He punched a dog to death in Chadwell Heath. To save a child, not for fun – though I dare say you could, back then. Had some stories, Ted. They'd come looming at you, out of these clouds of pipe smoke. Great wreaths of it. Never saw him without the pipe. That was sad, how *he* went.

She thrusts the bowl towards him.

Spicy Nik Nak?

OLI. Oh.

He takes some.

MARIANNE. Or I've wasabi peas out on the side. Bloody great jar. I get given them from one of the parents cos I go into the school over the road at Christmas and I'm afraid to open it or they go.

OLI. This is lovely.

MARIANNE. Now, let's see what you brought.

She picks up a bottle she'd evidently been handed when OLI *arrived. She squints at the label.*

OLI. I asked for a nice one.

MARIANNE. And that was a sweet thing to do. We'll open that later, I should think.

OLI. Bob Fraser's confirmed for the convention now. He emailed back today.

MARIANNE. Is he? That's interesting. Both days?

OLI. Yes.

MARIANNE. Can't be doing Chichester then. Not in Dominic's thing, anyway. Hmm. Maybe they *have* fallen out.

OLI. It's awesome that he's said yes! It makes it all, like, so much bigger.

The wrong thing to say.

MARIANNE. Does it?

OLI. I mean – that he's doing it and you are too. That he's doing it as well as you. That you're both, like, doing it together. Having you both is just, like, awesome. I mean, even if it was just you it'd – I don't mean *just* you – but even if it was, like, only you it'd still be amazing and awesome. It'd still be, like, the best thing ever!

MARIANNE. But now…?

OLI. Now it's – even more just totally… awesome.

MARIANNE *smiles*. OLI *takes a drink*.

MARIANNE. I'd like to see the adverts before they go out.

OLI *nods*.

I must think about what I'm going to wear.

OLI. We've got your dress from season three. The white silk one from 'To Disappear or Die'.

MARIANNE. Where's that come from?

OLI. Someone on one of the forums has it. That, Bob's jacket from 'The Screaming Mountain', and one of the Klaston's mutated hands from 'Frenzy of the Spheroids'.

MARIANNE. Well, I shan't be wearing that.

OLI. Oh, no – I didn't mean… We're going to display them.

MARIANNE. I'd look ridiculous, dolled up like that now.

OLI. No, no, of course.

Pause.

MARIANNE. The Screaming Mountain's what we used to call Owen from Wigs.

The doorbell rings.

Ooh, now, right!

She goes to the front door. Opens it. KATE is there and, behind her – younger, gorgeous SUZANNE.

KATE. Hello.

MARIANNE. Hello! Come in!

KATE. Marianne, you remember Suzanne.

SUZANNE. Hello again.

MARIANNE. I do, I do. Come in. Come in. Pop your coats
there by the door.

It's only now, as they move into the room, that they see OLI.

Let me get some glasses. We've opened a bottle already. In
anticipation!

She darts into the kitchen. KATE, SUZANNE *and* OLI *are
left with each other.*

OLI. Hello.

SUZANNE. Hello.

KATE. Hello…

OLI. I'm Oli.

SUZANNE. Suzanne.

They shake hands. MARIANNE *comes in with two more
champagne flutes. She pours as she speaks.*

MARIANNE. Kate, Suzanne – this is Oli. Oli – Suzanne and
Kate.

OLI. Hi.

KATE. Yes, we've just –

MARIANNE. So, now, there you go.

She hands a glass to SUZANNE. *Pours a second.*

A-n-d… There you are.

Hands a glass to KATE.

How are we doing?

She looks at her and OLI*'s glasses.*

Okay. Well. Cheers!

SUZANNE. Cheers!

OLI. Cheers!

They clink glasses. Sip.

A moment.

MARIANNE. Shall we sit down?

Please –

She indicates to SUZANNE, *who sits on the sofa, in the place* OLI *had been.*

How was the journey? What's it like outside?

OLI *dithers momentarily about sitting beside* SUZANNE, *but sees that* KATE *is intending that.*

I haven't been out today but it looks frightful.

Meanwhile, MARIANNE *has sat in the armchair. This leaves only a stool free.* OLI *sits on that.*

SUZANNE. No, it's fine, actually. It's quite mild, isn't it?

KATE. Yes.

MARIANNE. Oh, Oli, you need a cushion.

OLI. Oh, no, honest, I'm okay.

MARIANNE. No, no, no. Wait – Suzanne. There's a cushion behind you. Would you mind...?

SUZANNE. Oh –

SUZANNE *takes the cushion from behind her and passes it to him.*

MARIANNE. There you go. You'll be better with that.

OLI. Oh. Thank you.

He places it underneath him. It's a little too big for the stool and looks awkward.

MARIANNE. I've just been boring Oli senseless with all my old anecdotes.

OLI. Oh, no, not at all – !

KATE. Well, I'm glad you got them out of the way.

MARIANNE. Oli's a fan, Suzanne. Of – well. Of me!

SUZANNE. Gosh!

MARIANNE. There's a series I did, way back when. *Dark Sublime*. And it seems it has something of a – reach. Beyond the years. Oli's organising a convention.

SUZANNE. Really?

OLI. Not *just* me. I'm on the committee. I do the website.

SUZANNE. The committee!

KATE. In Walsall.

SUZANNE. Walsall?

MARIANNE. The hotel. Two days. Five hundred people!

SUZANNE. Blimey. Like a work conference?

KATE. I wouldn't have thought so.

MARIANNE. No! Much more fun than that.

OLI. We've got most of the main cast, and some of the production team, and some visual-FX guys, and there'll be, like, interview panels and a – a – cabaret, and we've got some stuff to auction, and there'll be, like, a showing of the whole series. Every episode.

KATE. Much more fun.

MARIANNE. It's for Cystic Fibrosis.

SUZANNE. Do you dress up?

OLI. No.

I mean, I guess, like, people can, if they want. It's not something I do.

SUZANNE. You see these costumes, don't you, sometimes, on the news. The trouble people go to! I always wonder if they travel like that or if they do it when they're there. In the toilets. I mean, you couldn't, could you? Some of them are so elaborate. It's not like touching up your lipstick. They must leave the house like that.

KATE. Pity the neighbours.

SUZANNE. I mean, you have to admire the effort.

OLI. It's not something I've ever been in to.

MARIANNE. No.

OLI. The thing with cosplay is, people only notice it if it's about science-fiction. Saturday afternoons, the terraces are full of grown men in costume.

MARIANNE. Ha!

SUZANNE. I'd never thought of it like that.

MARIANNE. They walk amongst us…

KATE. 'Cosplay'!

SUZANNE. Have you done one of these conferences before?

OLI. Convention? No.

SUZANNE. Convention, sorry.

KATE *points at* SUZANNE *in mock-admonishment at her faux pas.*

OLI. It probably wouldn't be happening if I hadn't met Marianne.

SUZANNE. Really?

OLI. Yeah, because… She's the star.

SUZANNE. Wow. Marianne – !

KATE *rolls her eyes.*

MARIANNE. How's *your* work, Suzanne? Work in a bank, don't you?

SUZANNE. Er, *for* a bank. It's not quite on the counter! It's – fine. Busy. As ever. I've got some leave to take, though I don't know when I'm going to do that. But – I survive.

KATE. What are we... Are we eating or, what's...

MARIANNE. I thought we'd just ring out for a Chinese or something. I didn't want to be stuck in the kitchen all night.

SUZANNE. Lovely.

OLI. Awesome.

MARIANNE. Is that all right?

KATE *hasn't answered and is instead giving* MARIANNE *a look ('Really?').*

SUZANNE. Have you done one of these – conventions before, Marianne?

MARIANNE. No, this'll be the first, believe it or not.

SUZANNE. I bet you're used to being stopped in the street though, aren't you?

MARIANNE. Oh, you know. It does happen, from time to time. Got it a lot when I was in *Emmerdale*.

SUZANNE (*keen*). Oh, yes, I –

MARIANNE. But people are generally nice. They just want to be able to say that they've met you. An autograph and a smile. If that's the price...

KATE. You're keeping Oli waiting for his.

MARIANNE. What?

KATE. Autograph.

MARIANNE. Oli's not 'people', are you, Oli?

OLI. Um –

SUZANNE. You're a big fan, are you, Oli? Of – what was it? *Dark...*?

OLI. *Sublime*. Yeah, massive.

SUZANNE. I don't think I've ever seen it.

OLI. It's really good. We're trying to get it released on DVD.

SUZANNE. Right. Gosh, you *are…*

Is this a – do you do this for a job?

OLI. No. No, I work at Waterstones.

SUZANNE. Oh, okay.

OLI. It's just, like, a – hobby.

SUZANNE. Right.

I paraglide.

OLI. Oh, wow.

SUZANNE. Sorry, I didn't mean for that to sound –

MARIANNE. Let's open a bottle, shall we? Oli, will you go and get some glasses? Wine glasses. They're in the cupboard above the Nutribullet.

OLI. Sure.

He heads to the kitchen.

SUZANNE. I might just nip to the bathroom…

MARIANNE. Of course. Through there, on the left.

MARIANNE and KATE are left alone. MARIANNE smiles at KATE.

KATE (*low*). What are you doing?

MARIANNE (*low*). What?

KATE (*low*). *Him.*

MARIANNE (*low*). What?

KATE (*low*). I thought tonight was about –

She gestures loosely, indicating SUZANNE and MARIANNE.

MARIANNE (*low*). It is!

KATE sighs in exasperation. MARIANNE frowns in exaggerated confusion (mouths 'What?').

OLI *enters with four wine glasses. He places them on the table.*

OLI. You look good in the photo.

It takes KATE *a moment to realise that he's addressing her.*

KATE. Me? What photo?

OLI. On the shelf.

He points.

MARIANNE. Oona's fortieth.

KATE*'s face is a study of incredulity.*

Pass me a bottle, Oli.

OLI. The one I brought?

MARIANNE. Um. Not yet. Let's have one from over there.

OLI *passes her a bottle of red wine.*

OLI. I mean, you look nice now, too.

KATE.... Thank you.

MARIANNE *unscrews the bottle and starts to pour.*

MARIANNE (*re: wine*). It's not as warm as it might be.

OLI. I love all the fashions from back then.

MARIANNE. They're all *back* in fashion now, aren't they?

OLI. You look so cool.

MARIANNE. There you go.

She hands OLI *a glass of wine.* SUZANNE *enters.*

OLI. Thank you.

MARIANNE. Kate.

MARIANNE *passes her a glass.*

OLI. Have you seen the picture of Kate, Suzanne?

KATE. N– no, she hasn't! This is the first time Suzanne's been here!

SUZANNE. What picture?

KATE. No picture. It doesn't matter.

MARIANNE. The one on the shelf there. It's Kate outside a club. Nothing controversial.

SUZANNE *sits back on the sofa.*

SUZANNE. I'll have a look at it later.

SUZANNE *reaches towards* KATE, *touches her leg, checking in.*

OLI *rubs his arm.*

MARIANNE. Suzanne.

MARIANNE *passes her a glass of wine.*

SUZANNE. Thank you.

MARIANNE. It's a touch on the cold side, I'm afraid.

SUZANNE. Oh, that's all right.

She takes a sip.

Very nice.

OLI. It's lovely.

SUZANNE. So, Kate was telling me you go back some way, you two.

MARIANNE. Was she?

Well, yes, we've put the hours in, haven't we?

KATE. You can say that again.

MARIANNE. Back when I was being wooed.

KATE. You what?

MARIANNE. That was how you met people back then – going to groups. The personal is political. All that. Lots of sitting in circles. Lots of lists!

KATE. There was a lot of good work done by those groups. A lot of *necessary* work.

MARIANNE. No, there was – but not a lot of *joie de vivre*, was there? Not a lot of laughter.

KATE. I think this is selective memory in operation. If we'd wanted hysterics we'd have asked you to read out your CV.

SUZANNE. Kate!

MARIANNE *seems to roll with* KATE*'s surprisingly low-blow.*

MARIANNE. Ooh! That's slander! It was my CV that provoked a bit of excitement in that group!

KATE. I don't think either the Women's Liberation Movement or the Labour Party were going to be excessively advantaged by coopting the star of *Bird in the Hand*.

MARIANNE (*to* OLI). That's exactly how they used to talk.

(*To* KATE.) It's precisely *because* I'd been in *Bird in the Hand* that I was seen as – beneficial.

KATE. Until we found out you were a fifth columnist.

MARIANNE (*mock horror*). What does *that* mean?!

KATE. No, okay, maybe not. Until the drink ran out then.

MARIANNE (*to* SUZANNE *and* OLI). That *is* fair.

(*To* KATE.) We had much more fun once I got you away from all that.

KATE. Is that what we did? I'll write that down.

MARIANNE (*to* SUZANNE). All the spines of my books were turning green. That was the warning sign.

KATE. You were never really an ally.

MARIANNE. Oi! I – fought fights. You didn't lead a TV series as a woman back then without having... 'robust conversations'. Still don't, I imagine. I did plenty. I just liked – living life.

SUZANNE. Are you working at the moment, Marianne?

MARIANNE. Er... I do these workshops – corporate training – when I'm between... I read a short story for Radio 4 a few weeks ago. That's what you're drinking.

But it's nice to have chance to catch your breath.

SUZANNE. I don't think it would suit me. The insecurity.

KATE. No.

SUZANNE. But the variety must be nice?

MARIANNE. Yes, you never quite know what you're going to be doing next.

Though Oli has a regular job and it's because of that that he found *me*.

SUZANNE. How come?

KATE (*nods at* MARIANNE). Historical fiction.

MARIANNE. While he was at work he bumped into another *Dark Sublime* alumnus – his first. Didn't you? (*To* KATE.) Maurice Bree.

KATE. The pederast?

MARIANNE. Well, we don't know.

KATE. Well, we *do*.

MARIANNE. Anyway, he conducted an interview with him –

KATE. Is that what the cushion's for?

MARIANNE. And – Kate! – that gave him the taste for, um... that gave him the idea to try and find the rest of us.

SUZANNE. Very industrious! And... you publish these, do you?

OLI. They're podcasts.

SUZANNE. Ah, right. (*To* MARIANNE.) And you've done one?

MARIANNE. I have.

SUZANNE. I'll have to have a listen. (*To* KATE.) We could do that on the way down next weekend.

KATE. That's… one of the options available to us.

MARIANNE. What's that?

SUZANNE. We're going to Bournemouth for the weekend.

MARIANNE. Are you?

SUZANNE. A friend at work recommended this little place and I need to use this leave up. We're both taking a half-day on Friday, so…

MARIANNE. Bournemouth.

I've toured there a few times. I wouldn't go mad.

KATE. We're not staying in the theatre.

SUZANNE. Just to see the sea, really.

KATE. It'll be nice.

SUZANNE. And I've a friend who runs a restaurant fairly nearby. So I think we'll pop in there.

KATE. Michelin star.

OLI. Wow.

SUZANNE. Just the one.

MARIANNE. You don't like all that stuff.

KATE. All what stuff?

MARIANNE. All that… fine dining.

KATE. Since when?

MARIANNE. You like – Oli, pass me your bottle.

He does. She unscrews, pours.

(*To* SUZANNE.) She spasms if you take her near Café Rouge.

KATE. 'Fine dining'? I *do* avoid Café Rouge. I avoid a specific branch of Café Rouge owing to the memory of an excruciating stand-up row about a mushroom risotto. *That* ring any bells?

MARIANNE. She can't abide *MasterChef*.

KATE (*sighs*). Marianne –

MARIANNE. You can't!

KATE. It wasn't *me* that went ballistic when I didn't get asked to do the voice-over!

MARIANNE. Oh, that was –

KATE. I like eating out.

MARIANNE. I'm saying nothing.

Suzanne, you're empty.

A beat. Then she gestures with the bottle.

SUZANNE. Oh, no, fine, thanks. Thank you. I'm not a fast drinker.

MARIANNE. Fast worker, though. Oli.

She hands him the bottle to pour himself. He tentatively pours a small amount into his glass, uncertain about the atmosphere.

SUZANNE. What do you mean?

KATE. Have you been drinking?

MARIANNE *exaggerates peering into her glass.*

I mean, before we arrived.

MARIANNE. Perhaps it's the sea. The sea, the sea! (*To* OLI.) That's where you're going wrong, you see. Landlocked, the Midlands.

KATE. Oh, I see…

MARIANNE. That's only a weekend, but… I think you put her off, Oli.

KATE. Marianne.

MARIANNE. I mean, I think you're nice but Kate's not so keen!

KATE. Marianne! Enough!

MARIANNE. He's nice!

A moment.

SUZANNE. Maybe I should –

KATE. I think we might go.

MARIANNE. I'm not saying anything wrong. You're going to Bournemouth – lovely. You're not going to Walsall. Fine. You'll have a nice time in Bournemouth. Suzanne's there.

She raises her glass in a toast.

Suzanne!

KATE. Marianne! Please.

MARIANNE. What?

KATE. You're being embarrassing!

MARIANNE (*to* OLI). Am I being embarrassing?

KATE. This is completely unnecessary –

MARIANNE. We haven't done anything in the last two years and now – Bournemouth!

KATE. Haven't done – ? I see you practically every week!

MARIANNE. We haven't been away!

KATE. No, we haven't! But – I mean, even if – ! I've been looking after my mum!

MARIANNE. But now you can drop everything and head to the seaside!

KATE. Can you hear yourself? This is excruciating!

MARIANNE. Don't give me notes!

KATE (*to* SUZANNE). I'm sorry about this.

SUZANNE (*quietly, to* KATE). I might nip outside –

SUZANNE *moves over to where their coats are hanging.*

MARIANNE. Don't apologise for me!

KATE. 'Don't' – ? I *will* because you're being completely unreasonable! This is rude and embarrassing, for *all* of us! And as for –

She points at OLI.

You're using him! That boy! He's here because he – God Almighty! – looks up to you! And you're throwing that back in his face! Now. *I've* seen you with a drink before –

MARIANNE. Don't patronise me!

KATE.…

We're going to go. You need to go to bed and wake up tomorrow morning and think abo–

MARIANNE. Piss off!

Pause.

KATE (*to* SUZANNE). Come on.

They walk to the door and collect their coats. SUZANNE *exits, but as* KATE *stands on the threshold she hesitates then comes back into the room.*

I am not your lover! I am not your lover! That's not who we are! And you need to get that into your head! You –

MARIANNE *opens her mouth to retort.*

How *dare* you – ! I haven't lost my temper in…

She stops, and heads for the door.

MARIANNE. Well…

KATE. You did this! *You* did this!

One fucking star!

She exits.

MARIANNE *and* OLI *are left.*

KATE *comes back in.*

(*To* OLI.) You should go home.

She exits.

OLI *is unsure of the right thing to do. He picks up his jacket.*

OLI. Um.

MARIANNE *looks at him.*

ACT TWO

Scene One

Walsall. A hotel function room. A banner reads 'RubyCon 1'.

The Dark Sublime *theme fades as* OLI *enters – lanyard, clipboard, handheld mic.*

OLI. Okay, hello, everyone. Hello. Hello.

The mic isn't working. He looks to his left, receiving offstage instruction.

Hello-o-o, hello-o-o, hello.

He shakes his head. Looks at the bottom of the mic, flicks a switch.

Hello, hello.

Still nothing. Flicks the switch again. This time the mic works.

Hello, hell– ah! Okay! Got there in the end. Right, hi guys. Welcome to RubyCon! RubyCon One. My name's Oli, I'm one of the organisers. I run DSOnline-dot-com, that I know many of you will have, like, er, visited… And thank you for making it the premier, dedicated *Dark Sublime* website! Thanks to the guys for putting that set of clips together. Awesome stuff. Just a taste of what's coming up over the weekend! Er, I'm just going to run through the day's events – there's been a couple of amendments to the schedules, the ones in your packs, so, um… okay. In a moment we've got the Directors' Panel with Douglas Graham and Richard Bryant. This is now the *only* panel Richard will be appearing on this weekend. As some of you might know, Richard is now a Humanist minister and is actually conducting a wedding this afternoon, so we're very grateful that he's found time to fit us in at all. Then, after the panel, Douglas and Richard will be signing autographs. That'll be at the far end of the breakfast bar, but, please – it's *one* autograph and *one* selfie per person. Richard's got to get away fairly quickly so I'm afraid we have to be strict. The stewards *will* be enforcing that. Okay? Then there's lunch from twelve-thirty to two, followed by, *at* two, a screening of an early edit of the pilot episode – now, this is *not* the version screened by UK Gold in 2006. This is a previously unseen edit, recently unearthed by the BFI, and I think there might be one or two surprises in store for anyone who's familiar with the design of the Council Chamber from the end of series one.

He hears a gasp.

Oh yeah! Oh yeah! Then that's followed –

He glances into the wings.

Oh, so – I've – er, I've been asked to say that the Shadow Ruby tracking panel down here – (*Gestures.*) You're welcome to take selfies by it – that's, like, what it's there for – but people have been, like, snapping bits off it. Now, firstly, that's just not a nice thing to do, and, secondly, it's, like, a *replica*, built and loaned to us by Simon MacColl. It's *not* the original panel from the series. It's *not* the original. All you're doing is making Simon take another trip to Homebase. So, you know – come on, guys.

Right.

He consults the schedule.

So, the screening at two. That's followed at three o'clock by our star panel: Bob Fraser. Brian Scarborough. Maurice Bree. Yvette Neil. George Cook. Wendy O'Hara. And, making her first *Dark Sublime*-related public appearance since the 1980 Thames Telethon – it's Marianne Hogg! Yes! Star of *Emmerdale*, *Bird in the Hand*, and many, many more, we're incredibly honoured to have Marianne here this weekend – and, as a friend, I'm very grateful to her for having agreed to attend. If you've ever seen, like, clips of Marianne being interviewed – and there's a whole page of links on the website – then you'll know we're in for a treat!

I know. Sick.

Then – right – just to say: there's an obvious misprint, I'm sure you've all figured out: at eleven, Kit Purdie-Smith's talk in Room Three is on special *effects*. Your schedules should, of course, read S*F*X Talk, not S*E*X Talk –

He responds to laughter.

Yeah, yeah. I said I'd be happy to proofread them but I was told…

Anyway. I'm going to hand over to Tom now, who's going to introduce the first of our panels. There might be a moment or two while we get everything sorted, so, just, please, bear with us.

Cool.

He checks with his offstage help – 'Turn the mic off?' Okay.

Scene Two

The grounds of Alexandra Palace, North London. A summer's day – blue sky, sun, a slight bite to the breeze. Sitting on the grass: KATE *and* SUZANNE.

KATE. It's marvellous here. I feel so calm and relaxed.

SUZANNE. I love that view. London, spread out before you. You could reach out and grab it.

KATE. Spoken like a banker.

SUZANNE. Hey!

They're smiling. Looking out across the city. It's all very light.

I was at school with an Alexandra Harris.

KATE. What's that got to do with the price of fish?

SUZANNE. Alexandra Palace.

KATE. Oh, I see.

It's an oblique link and KATE *does with it what she can.*

Oh, wasn't last weekend lovely?

SUZANNE. Wasn't it.

KATE. Really lovely.

God, we did well with the weather.

The puddings!

SUZANNE. Hm!

KATE *can't quite relax – starts looking at her legs, flexing her foot, her calves.*

've you got cramp?

KATE. No. Just looking at my legs. Cursing my mother for her varicose veins.

SUZANNE. There's nothing wrong with your legs.

KATE. You're very kind but that's a lie.

SUZANNE. We've all got something.

KATE. D'you think?

SUZANNE. Mmm.

My hips could act as flood defences.

KATE. Don't be silly!

SUZANNE. And that's okay. I've come to an accommodation with them now. I rather like them.

KATE. Don't be silly. You look lovely.

SUZANNE. Thank you. I think so too.

KATE. Oh, it's nice to just…

SUZANNE. I love Saturdays. Saturday afternoons. Like this.

KATE. Yes.

Pause.

I've got a man coming round next weekend to sort out my overflow pipe.

SUZANNE. That's nice.

KATE *laughs.*

KATE. Sorry, it just popped into my head. It's been dripping since Good Friday. I'm sleeping with these earplugs – what are they called? Like plasticine. Have you seen them? They're ever so good.

SUZANNE. Kate.

KATE. Swimmers use them, apparently. Says so on the packet. Silicon. What?

SUZANNE. Sssh.

KATE. Sorry.

SUZANNE *reaches out her hand, finds* KATE*'s. Holds it.*

There's barely a cloud.

I must take that gammon out of the freezer.

I should book an appointment, really. I keep meaning to have them done. They're not playing up or anything, but – or maybe that ship's sailed. Bit late in the day for anything like that now.

KATE *takes a pack of cigarettes from her bag, takes out a cigarette. Stops. Puts the cigarette back in the packet.*

These are increasingly more of a – hindrance. I should give up. Shall I give up? Is summer a good time to give up? Be Christmas soon, and they do help then. Then it's New Year – which is when everyone says they're giving up, so I can't do it then and retain any credibility. I'll give up now. There – I've given up!

She pops the packet back into her bag with a flourish.

Beat.

It's very calming, being with you.

SUZANNE. You wouldn't tell.

KATE *laughs. She knows she's being ridiculous.*

KATE. There's a new meeting room, up on the fifth floor at
work. Glass panels, you know. Modern. And each panel's got
someone on it, from different departments. Internal. They've
had these transfers done – at god knows what cost. That's
verboten to ask. It's meant to be terribly egalitarian. 'This is
us.' That kind of thing. And over two of these panels is this
bloody great picture of Tony Meakin, Head of Comms – with
some asinine soundbite picked out in a drop-shadow font,
some life-sapping platitude – so at least it's genuinely
representative – and I'm not kidding, but you think they'd've
photoshopped out his ear hair, wouldn't you? No. So when
you're in there for the umpteenth round of back-and-forth
about who's cutting what from where you can see whoever's
sitting opposite slowly adjusting their position so they can
line it up with the head of the person facing them and give
them a new hair-do.

We all call it The Salon.

Head of Comms!

SUZANNE. We just have glass. Quotes are passé.

KATE. Ah, you're money, though. That's the difference. We're
'working together'...

You never really talk about work, do you?

SUZANNE. No. When I'm not there, I'm not there.

KATE. That's good. That's a good...

I think about it too much, really.

Look at those sweet peas.

SUZANNE. There's more to life than work.

KATE. Well, as I say – *you're* in money.

SUZANNE. Are you worried about something? Work's all right, isn't it?

KATE. Oh, yeah, yeah. It's retirement I'm thinking about.

Pause.

SUZANNE. Have you spoken to Marianne?

No reply.

Have you?

KATE. Who?

She's at that event this weekend.

SUZANNE. You need to speak to her.

KATE. I know.

I know.

SUZANNE. She'll be feeling worse than you.

KATE. *You* don't know her very well!

Oh, she's an idiot!

She sighs.

SUZANNE. I feel for her.

KATE. Do you?

SUZANNE. All that time. Not saying anything.

KATE. We're friends!

SUZANNE. Wouldn't be the first.

KATE. We're also ancient!

SUZANNE. What's age got to do with anything?

KATE. I don't know.

I thought – if I ever thought about us talking about it, in the past – I thought it would feel...

Oh, I don't know *what* I thought!

I don't suppose I ever thought we *would* end up talking about it, really.

SUZANNE. You knew, then?

KATE. She's not *that* good an actress!

I just didn't think she'd be…

SUZANNE. What?

KATE. Like that.

Petty.

It's beneath her. It's beneath *me*!

I mean, what did she imagine she was going to achieve? How old are we, for Christ's sake? You'd think we were teenagers! How's she got the energy?!

And… Now what?

SUZANNE. Now what.

KATE. Well, now, *I* have to be the bigger person, don't I? Obviously. I have to say 'It's all right, let's forget about it, let's move on', don't I?

SUZANNE. And that's not how you feel…?

KATE. I don't know how I feel! I feel – angry that I have to *think* about how I feel!

That's what work's for – conscious relationships with people! Negotiating with idiots that you're glad to be shot of, come the end of the day! Friends are meant to be different! When I'm with friends I don't want to – ! I just want a chat and a laugh. I shouldn't have to *think*!

SUZANNE *smiles*.

You know what I mean.

SUZANNE. I do.

KATE. I'm allowed to be cross!

SUZANNE. Of course you are.

Pause.

KATE. I'm not an idiot. I haven't been blind to it all. It's just...

She's never... It's always been...

SUZANNE. Unspoken?

KATE. Yes.

And... Low.

I've known her almost forty years.

SUZANNE. And then I came along.

KATE. I have had *other* relationships!

SUZANNE. How was she with them?

KATE *considers*.

KATE. Cold.

SUZANNE. Was she?

KATE. Mm. Oh, I mean – not to the outside eye. But you could tell. *I* could.

SUZANNE. Was she one of them?

KATE *looks at her.*

'Other relationships'?

KATE. Oh. No!

No, not – really.

Oh, look, it needed to be said, I suppose. It's not a healthy – thing, is it?

Is it?

SUZANNE. I think – love is... rare enough, that it needs... cherishing, wherever it flowers.

Beat.

KATE. You must stand out like a sore thumb in the financial sector.

SUZANNE *laughs*.

Did they slip something in that camomile tea in the café?

SUZANNE. The world's full of people who don't get on. You work with them. I'm related to them. Marianne loves you. And I know why she does. I've spent enough time with you. I… understand that feeling.

She's never assaulted you, has she?

KATE. Only artistically.

SUZANNE. Well, then.

KATE. You feel… observed, you know? You're being looked at – watched – in a way that isn't… normal. That's the thing. I don't want to be 'looked at'! That's her line – she's the bloody actress! That's probably why she thinks it's fine. She enjoys it, so she thinks I do too!

SUZANNE. I doubt she thinks about it like that.

KATE. It's that boy. I knew he was bad news.

SUZANNE. It's not his fault.

KATE. Isn't it? Feeding her ego. They're mad, these people. This unhealthy fixation with the past!

SUZANNE. He seemed rather sweet to me.

KATE. Why doesn't anyone write to *me*? I've staved off the best part of sixty grand's worth of cuts to core services over the past eighteen months! Why doesn't anyone want *my* autograph?

SUZANNE. You'd hate it if they did.

KATE. Yes, I would.

Oh – !

Pause.

But *you're* not cross?

SUZANNE. No. It wasn't about me.

KATE. You're very different people.

Which I suppose is the problem.

Or not.

I don't know.

Does anything make you angry?

SUZANNE *thinks*.

SUZANNE. I marched against the war in Iraq.

KATE. Talk about putting it in perspective.

Pause.

They do that thing sometimes, don't they, in Sunday supplements and the like – 'Letter to My Younger Self'. Mine'd say: stay away from actors.

SUZANNE. Come on. You've had some good parties out of it, I bet.

KATE. Not really. You tend to have to watch a play beforehand and nobody wants that.

SUZANNE. It's nice to hear you talk about it. Hear what you're thinking.

KATE. Oh, I'm sorry. I wasn't – I didn't want to spoil the weekend. That's all.

I'm always talking about her, somehow. I wanted the weekend to be about *us*.

SUZANNE. And it was. I appreciate you thinking like that. But she obviously matters to you, so… I don't mind hearing about her.

KATE. Start the clock! I want to see how long it takes before you go back on that.

SUZANNE. Well… I don't mean to the exclusion of everything else.

KATE. No. See. You're regretting it already.

SUZANNE. I'm a little envious, truth be told.

KATE. Of what?

SUZANNE. You two. I've never had a friend like that.

KATE. No. They're in short supply, I hope.

SUZANNE. You laugh, but they are!

The two of you, I can see…

The warp and weft of you. You're tied to each other. My friends – we're… I mean, we're… Don't get me wrong, we see each other, we have nice times. But we're not…

You and Marianne are like different sides of the same coin.

KATE. Hmm. I'm tails.

SUZANNE. You can only joke like that because you know I'm right.

KATE *smiles, wanting to hear more*.

I'm happy. I genuinely am. It's taken a while, but I am, now. Too old not to be! No, I am! And I've no regrets. That's important. But if I've got a… wish? I wish I'd had the sort of relationship with someone that you and Marianne have.

I really like me, and I wish I could have shared that with someone.

KATE. Oh – ! Suzanne – !

SUZANNE. It's all right!

Beat. KATE *is overwhelmed by* SUZANNE*'s easy candour*.

KATE. *I'd* like to share it with you.

SUZANNE (*smiling*). It's not the same thing – but, yes.

KATE. I don't want to be…

SUZANNE. What?

KATE. Well. I don't want to – I don't know. Hold you back. I'm conscious that – you know. I'm *older* than –

SUZANNE. Hey. We've talked about this.

KATE. I know. But.

SUZANNE. You and I will never have what you and Marianne have. But we'll have what *we* have. And that's what I want.

KATE. Okay. As long as you...

SUZANNE. I'm *your* fan.

KATE. Oh, don't say that! That word is banned!

SUZANNE. All right. (*Beat.*) But I am.

And you're mine, I hope.

KATE *smiles.*

KATE. Maybe *we* should go to a hotel and show our appreciation for each other.

I mean – again.

SUZANNE. I'm not saying I've got all the answers. I haven't. But I feel like I've identified the right questions.

KATE *sighs.*

KATE. I used to think this would all get easier.

They look out over the city.

SUZANNE. It's funny thinking about television starting here, isn't it? Not all that long ago. Beaming out over those streets. The city.

Feels so – fragile, somehow.

KATE. What, was that here?

SUZANNE. Yes. That mast.

She looks behind her.

There's a plaque. I was reading it while you were back there separating that Cocker Spaniel and the Miniature Schnauzer.

KATE. Got no thanks for that either!

Oh, I try not to think about television. It's a little too present in my life.

SUZANNE. Must have been so odd, that first time. Switching it on. Suddenly, a stranger, there, in the front room. The parlour!

KATE. They had it lucky. It was just an illusion for them.

Pause.

SUZANNE. Send her a text at least.

KATE. Maybe. Maybe.

Anyway, what was that about 'understanding the feeling'?

SUZANNE. Oh, that.

She leans over and kisses KATE, *unhurried, meant. A smile.*

Scene Three

Darkness.

The blinking lights of KOSLEY – *but flickering, straining to transmit. He speaks over a bed of increasing static.*

KOSLEY (*voice-over*). Vision on! Sound on!

Commander!

My detectors indicate a mighty maze of mystic magic rays is all about us in the blue!

Commander!

In sight and sound they trace living pictures out of space!

Commander, are you receiving me?

This could be important! Living pictures, Commander!

Commander!

Commander!?!

Scene Four

The convention – towards midnight.

A conference room. Stacked chairs. A whiteboard leans against a wall.

From outside, the sound of the bar – a hubbub of noise and gaiety.

MARIANNE *enters. No one here – relief! She takes a moment. Enjoys the silence.*

OLI *enters.*

MARIANNE *laughs – of course he does! But* OLI *hadn't seen her, so this takes him by surprise.*

OLI. Oh. Hi.

MARIANNE. Am I needed?

OLI. No. I was just…

An awkward hiatus.

Are you okay?

MARIANNE. Yes. Fine.

OLI. Right.

Pause.

MARIANNE. I need five minutes, Oli.

OLI. Oh. Right. Sure.

Would you like a drink?

MARIANNE. No, I –

Oh, maybe I would. I'll have –

OLI. Brandy?

MARIANNE.… Yes.

I'll have a brandy. Yes.

OLI. No sweat.

She reaches for her bag.

MARIANNE. I'll give you some money…

OLI. No, no, no. It's fine.

MARIANNE. Are you sure?

But he's gone.

She takes her phone from her bag and – no.

She puts it back in the bag.

She looks round the room. Christ.

She takes one of the chairs from the stack and sits.

From her bag she takes a small paper bag of sweets. She pops one into her mouth.

OLI *comes back in carrying two brandies and his bag.*

OLI. Here we go.

He hands her a drink.

MARIANNE. Thanks.

OLI. Cheers.

MARIANNE *raises her glass in answer. They drink. It's* OLI*'s first brandy – he hopes he's covered that.*

George Cook's doing magic tricks out there.

MARIANNE. These places.

OLI. Conventions?

MARIANNE. Hotels. Like this.

This is where people come to die.

OLI. Off the A34?

MARIANNE. Yes – off the A34!

OLI. They did us a good deal cos of the Bank Holiday.

Pause. She offers him the paper bag.

MARIANNE. Foam banana?

OLI. Oh, er –

He takes one. She puts the paper bag back in her bag.

OLI *taps at his phone.*

It's buzzing out there! We could go back outside.

To the bar.

If you like.

It's going really well. You're a big hit.

MARIANNE. Am I?

OLI. Seriously? You were slaughtering everyone out there! That story about the scene-shifters' strike and the polystyrene cock...

MARIANNE. Thank god it was Princess Margaret. She could take things like that in her stride.

OLI. Hilarious!

MARIANNE. Oh... Oli!

You feel so – fraudulent.

OLI. Do you? Why?

OLI *takes a chair from the stack and sits.*

He taps at his phone. Each time it's brisk, quick, his attention returning to her.

MARIANNE. Stories. Anecdotes. Talking about... games we played in rehearsals. Rehearsals were... thirty-five years ago! Games we played thirty-five years ago! You weren't even born!

Sorry, I've said that before. Ha!

I'm boring myself.

From the bar outside – laughter.

OLI. Everyone's really impressed that I – that you're here. You've been the highlight of the weekend.

He taps at his phone.

MARIANNE. There's an epitaph!

OLI. We've raised loads.

MARIANNE. How much?

OLI. Well, we've got to add up, like, the final amounts from the auction… But – at least three grand.

MARIANNE. *Three thousand pounds?*

OLI. Yeah.

MARIANNE. Well, there's that, at least.

OLI *taps at his phone.*

What *are* you doing?

Dead in his tracks.

Tapping away incessantly. Like a tic!

OLI. Sorry. It's the Twitter feed.

MARIANNE. Feed is right. Voracious!

OLI. Sorry. I'll just…

He taps away, staccato. Pockets the phone.

There.

MARIANNE. Go out and do…

She gestures.

Whatever. If you want.

OLI. No, it's fine.

MARIANNE. Is it?

OLI. Yeah.

Pause.

OLI *is very consciously not pulling out his phone.*

Is it nice, seeing everyone again?

MARIANNE. If you were thirty years older you'd realise the redundancy of that question.

Pause.

OLI. I thought – maybe – I'd upset you earlier.

MARIANNE. What?

OLI. Before the cabaret.

MARIANNE. What are you talking about?

OLI. When you were chatting to Nick.

MARIANNE. Which one's Nick?

OLI. Teeth.

She thinks.

MARIANNE. He was telling me about damp-proofing! He's got a business! I'm getting him to look at my south-facing walls!

OLI. Oh.

MARIANNE. I signed this – you can hardly call it a painting – for him and he's going to do it gratis!

OLI. Oh, right.

MARIANNE. Do you know how much damp-proofing costs?

OLI. No.

MARIANNE. No!

Why do you think I was upset? Because I wasn't talking to you for five minutes?

OLI. No.

OLI *glances at his phone.*

They're all wondering where we are.

MARIANNE. Let them.

You can go.

OLI. S'okay.

Pause.

MARIANNE. Listen –

Um…

That night at my flat…

OLI. Oh, it's okay.

MARIANNE. No, I –

OLI. You – you don't have to –

MARIANNE. You don't know what I'm going to say!

…

I don't know what I'm going to say.

I'm obviously going to say – I'm sorry. You shouldn't have… I'm sorry that you – were there for that.

OLI. Yes. Yes.

MARIANNE. So…

OLI. It's fine.

The guy from the BFI's really impressed.

MARIANNE.…Is he?

OLI. Yeah. He came along cos they leant us the pilot. He says he's not a fan, but he knows a hell of a lot about the design of the Biocluster Helix. He's got photos of it being reused on the Kenny Everett Show.

MARIANNE *absorbs this as best she can*.

MARIANNE. Where's your friend? Josh.

OLI. Joel.

MARIANNE. Joel.

Is he not here? I thought he might have been here.

OLI. No. He, uh –

MARIANNE. Didn't want to come? Something of a shibboleth
for friendship, Walsall.

OLI. He, um...

(Huh!)

MARIANNE. You don't have to tell me. None of my business.

OLI. No. Um.

I asked him if he wanted to go out with me. And he, um.
Didn't.

MARIANNE. Ah.

OLI. He said he'd rather we stayed friends.

MARIANNE. Mm. Well –

OLI. And I thought, okay. Friends. Right. But... I've been
thinking about him for, like, the last year. Every day, for the
last year. And I've been wanting to ask him out since
November. Nine months! Well, I've been wanting to ask him
out since I first saw him but it was around November when
I realised, like, I *had* to. That I couldn't not any more. So I did.

And I felt like a twat when he said no. I mean, he didn't say
'no', he said he was flattered and... la la la and...

And I *did* give it a go. I tried, for, like, a week after. I thought,
maybe you can do this, you know. Maybe it's okay. And
I realised I couldn't. Not when – I was just, like, thinking
about him. All the time. Last thing at night. First thing in the
morning. Every single minute in-between. That's... You can't
be friends like that, can you?

He takes his phone from his pocket – tap-tap-tap, in reply,
then back into his pocket. Three seconds.

So I'd made up my mind anyway. But then he tells me –
this is, like, three weeks later – he's going on a date with

this other lad we know. And, I'm not being funny but – this guy. You wouldn't look at him twice. I'm not saying *I'm* all that, but… And he's into all the same stuff – the same music and… TV, and, like… I mean – he's just like *me*! So, you think – well, *thanks*. You could have had me, you could have had *me*, who you say you really like and get on with, but instead you choose this kind of weird fucking… parody!

I mean, I'd made up my mind already. That just proved I was right.

MARIANNE. What did you do?

OLI. Told him. Said we couldn't be friends. Said I didn't want to be just his friend.

MARIANNE.…

OLI. I can't live my life like that. He's all I've thought about for the last year. He's *all* I've thought about. I can't walk round with that inside me. If we're in my room, watching, like, an episode or something, I'd always be thinking – I want to kiss you. Or, why won't you hold my hand. I'm not doing that. It's not fair on *me*! Life's too short.

Aw, man. Sorry. Didn't mean to go on like that. Lame!

Pause. What to say?

MARIANNE *opens her mouth to reply –*

And a giant green lobster-like monster bursts into the room, claws snapping! Snap! Snap!

OLI *leaps up!*

Not in here! No! This room is out of bounds! Back into the public area, please! Back! Out! Out! Thank you! Thank you!

The monster is ushered out. OLI *closes the door.*

Idiots. Sorry about that.

He sits back down.

He smiles at MARIANNE, *trying to reestablish where they were.*

MARIANNE. You're very brave, you know.

OLI. Aw, no sweat. I think he was looking for the gents'.

MARIANNE....No, not *that* – ! I mean – !

OLI. Oh, right. Yeah.

He shrugs.

S'just how it is.

I mean, I've never even touched him and I know for a fact that he's let Damien Gilbey wank him off. Twice!

Sorry. Too much information.

I was talking to Kieron earlier. He was telling me about this staircase he's designed in this, like, museum in Spain. I'd never really thought about that before. The way light interacts with it. The space around it. It was really interesting.

MARIANNE. Who's Kieron?

OLI. Maurice's partner.

With the moustache. Green suit.

MARIANNE. *Maurice's* partner? I thought he was – I don't know *who* I thought he was.

OLI. Yeah. They've been together twenty-one years.

MARIANNE. Have they?

OLI. I thought he might, like, make a joke about that. Cos I'm twenty-one. But he didn't.

MARIANNE. Have they. Maurice.

OLI. I liked that.

I might learn Spanish.

MARIANNE. Christ, Oli!

OLI. What?

MARIANNE. You!

'Life's too short'!

From outside, the Dark Sublime *theme tune.*

OLI. Well, it is, isn't it? I respect myself more than that.

MARIANNE. That bloody music.

OLI. There's an all-night screening. All three series.

MARIANNE. You not going?

OLI. I can watch it any time.

MARIANNE *looks at her empty glass.*

Oh.

OLI *rummages in his bag, pulls out a small bottle of brandy. Offers it to her.*

Here you go.

MARIANNE. You're very well prepared.

She pours herself a glass.

OLI. I remember you saying how difficult it is to get drinks from hotels late at night.

MARIANNE. When did I say that?

OLI. 1989. On *Wogan.*

She hands him the bottle. He pours himself a glass.

Outside: radiophonic throb.

Do you remember being on location for 'Terror of the Gannetrids'?

MARIANNE. Oh, Christ – !

OLI. What?

MARIANNE. Of all the – !

It paid the mortgage – *helped* pay the mortgage – but it's not the – one bright book of life! I've played parts – over the

whole of my career – Portia! Rosalind! I played Hedda
Gabler at the Bolton Octagon and it was wonderful!
Truthful! It *meant* something. But this?

It doesn't mean anything! It. Doesn't. Mean. Anything.

You're twenty-one! You work in a bookshop! For the love of
Christ – read some fucking *books*!

I'm sorry. It's just –

Oh god.

Walsall!

*A terrible silence, punctuated by the muffled soundtrack from
outside ('No! No! No! (Scream.)')*

VYKAR *enters – no, not* VYKAR. *Stouter, less dynamic –
the actor who played* VYKAR, BOB FRASER.

BOB. Here you are, darling! We wondered where you'd got to.
They were going to close the bar but I've had a word. Got
another fifteen minutes or so, but it probably pays not to
hang around. Dougie's getting a round in – hold the front
page! And, frankly, the patience is starting to wear thin in
terms of answering questions about quarries. So – I said I'd
come and find you.

Everything all right?

MARIANNE. Bob, yes. Fine. I was just – taking a breather.

BOB. Ah, *that's* why you're hiding in here. Yes, I know what
you mean. Can get a bit much, can't it?

He glances at OLI.

MARIANNE (*to* BOB). You've met Oli?

BOB*'s attention has moved on.* OLI *had half-risen from his
seat but sits back down.*

BOB. I tell you what I wasn't expecting – surprising amount of
skirt out there. Thought it was going to be all BO and
bummers. Which it mainly is, of course, but still. You want to
look lively! We can both make hay if we put our minds to it.

Give 'em five minutes' blather on Teddington High Street
1981 and they're putty in your hands. Take it from me! What
do they say these days – nom nom nom?

He smacks his lips.

MARIANNE. Bob!

BOB. Shall we?

MARIANNE. Five minutes, Bob. Don't worry about a drink.
(To OLI.) Do you want one?

BOB. Nonsense! What's that? Brandy? Brandy – to make you
feel randy! I'll give you five and then come looking!

He exits.

MARIANNE. He's had two wives walk out on him. You can
see why, can't you?

Pause.

Three thousand pounds is amazing. You should be proud.

Don't sulk.

OLI. They were saying the same out there. Yvette Neil was
going on about how dated it is. Really going on. That's why
I came in here.

And I know it is, sometimes. I'm not stupid. I know it can be
sexist, and… homophobic, and… I know 'The Tentacles of
Rajput Janwari' would literally never be made now – but
that's cos it was 1979! A hundred – *ages* ago!

But it's – better than that! You know! It's like… The whole
message of the show is that things can change. Life isn't set.
And that's, like – !

And, you know – I've made friends from being into it –
proper friends! And it's made me aware of all sorts of stuff,
like, I know about… Buddhism! The Aztecs! Er… C. S.
Lewis! – because they were referenced in the programme!
I bought a poetry book cos it had the Auden poem in it, and
that got me into Philip Larkin, and they're fucking awesome!
I love those poems! So… you know.

MARIANNE. Well.

I mean – that is… great to hear. It is. And surprising, too. But –

OLI. What should I have watched instead? Or done? Why is it so – risible? You were *in* it!

MARIANNE. That's no guarantee of quality. I'm in this hotel.

OLI. Everyone takes the piss!

MARIANNE. Maybe it's jealousy.

OLI. What?

MARIANNE. Oh, I don't know, Oli. There's beggary in the love that can be reckoned.

The thing is… It's a television programme. It's a – fixed thing. So – you get the same enjoyment watching it now as you did when you first saw it. It can never disappoint. That's powerful. People, though. They change. They disappoint.

It's why I've spent my entire life in fiction. Hm!

Was it Eliot who said 'humans cannot bear very much reality'? I think it was. I think it was him. Him, or the casting director on *Holby City*. I forget.

Pause.

OLI. Were you… You didn't agree to meet me…

MARIANNE. What?

OLI. To get at your friend.

MARIANNE. No!

I wasn't planning to 'get' at my – at Kate at all. Christ, I have enough difficulty working out how to control the central heating, let alone concoct some elaborate bloody sting!

I'd had a drink and I was… sad. Ha! And that is all you need, let me tell you. A bullet and a gun.

It wasn't you.

From outside, a stab of synthesised incidental music.

It's been a long day.

Dougie Graham was chanting all through lunch and it wore me down a bit.

OLI. Does he really do that?

MARIANNE. Don't let him sell you one of his CDs.

Pause.

OLI. Do you love Kate?

No one has ever asked this question outright before.

MARIANNE....Of course.

OLI. I mean –

MARIANNE. I know what you mean.

Ohhhhhhhh – !

It's funny. In many ways, I don't. The way you mean. Not any more. We've known each other too long. I don't think I'd actually like to... And it wouldn't work, anyway. But... I did for so long that –

OLI. You're...

You're really important to me.

MARIANNE. Oli!

OLI. No, I know you're just an actor, but – you're not. You're more than that. Even the dull episodes are worth watching because you're in them. Whenever I've felt, like – sad, over the years – I've put an episode on and felt – better. I have! I felt better, watching you, and you had no idea. And I want you to know. Life's shit. Life's *shit*. And you're not shit. You're, like, the opposite of shit.

Pause.

MARIANNE. That's the best review I've ever had.

She sighs.

What time is it?

She checks her watch.

OLI. I think we're on the same train back tomorrow afternoon.

I thought. Like. If you wanted. We could get something to eat when it gets in. Wahaca or somewhere. Pizza Express. Wherever.

MARIANNE. Um. Let's see.

OLI. Okay. Sure. Course.

He rubs his arm.

Some of the guys are going back too so I could, like, always go off with them.

Nando's or something.

MARIANNE. I think I'll probably go straight home.

Outside: the squawk! of a radiophonic bird.

I'm actually going to be busy for a while, Oli. I'm not meant to say, but – I'm going into *EastEnders*. Christine. Environmental Health. Three episodes. Well, two episodes and a Red Button.

OLI. Wow. Great.

MARIANNE. So...

Outside: another squawk!

OLI. I was speaking to a guy earlier from a video production company. Poptropica. They do Value Added Material for DVDs and Blu-Rays. You know, special features and stuff. Like, documentaries and interviews. They need a runner. So, like, *I'm* going to be busy too.

Outside: another squawk!

MARIANNE. You should be out there, shagging your way from room to room.

OLI. So should you.

She smiles. Cheeky sod.

MARIANNE. You're twenty-one. Don't waste it!

OLI. No one I fancy.

MARIANNE. Lucky you.

I'm going to bed. Thank you for –

She holds up her glass, meaning that, then gestures with it to include the room ('everything'). Then raises it in a toast.

The Aztecs!

She goes to the door. She turns to say something.

OLI *is glancing at his phone. She leaves.* OLI *looks up. He is alone.*

OLI. Shit.

Outside: a radiophonic klaxon burst into life!

Suddenly, VYKAR *– and it is VYKAR, not* BOB FRASER *– bursts in, followed by* JAYLIN. *They are both carrying Mazon blasters.*

They appear not to see OLI, *whose eyes are like saucers.*

JAYLIN. They're bound to search in here!

VYKAR (*taking in the room*). This is where I asked Kosley to put us down.

JAYLIN. So now what?

VYKAR. Ssshh!

JAYLIN. Commander!

VYKAR. I'm trying to think!

No one's ever breached her citadel before. She's vulnerable. That gives us the advantage!

JAYLIN *looks around with disdain.*

JAYLIN. You call being here having the advantage?

VYKAR. Now, she needs this 'Shadow Ruby' to make the leap over into our dimension. That's going to be her priority. So, ours is to stop her getting it.

JAYLIN. And to rescue the President.

VYKAR. Well, of course!

This is an awful place.

JAYLIN. It's light years from the nearest civilised planet. It wasn't marked on any of the star charts.

VYKAR. What would compel anyone to come here?

VYKAR*'s wrist communicator beeps.*

KOSLEY (*voice-over*). Commander –

VYKAR. Not now, Kosley!

JAYLIN. But we don't know what the Shadow Ruby looks like.

VYKAR. I'm rather hoping – like a big red stone.

JAYLIN. I don't think it's going to be that simple.

VYKAR. No... Can't you sense it? If it's here it must be giving off some kind of... energy? Some signal?

KOSLEY (*voice-over*). Commander – (*Unintelligible static.*)

VYKAR. Kosley, shush!

JAYLIN. I've been trying to use my powers. But being so close to a breach between dimensions is causing sensory instability. It's making me feel a bit ill, if you must know.

VYKAR. It must be shrouded in some way...

KOSLEY (*voice-over*). Commander, please – !

VYKAR. Kosley! Not now! We're trying to hide!

I've got a bit of a headache myself. I assumed it was just the lack of air in these tunnels.

JAYLIN. It's more than that. This place reeks of death.

VYKAR. It worries me that Kosley put us down in the wrong place. He doesn't usually make that kind of mistake.

JAYLIN. I don't think he could help it. We're in an entirely different reality. It would have affected his calculations. None of the parallels run quite true.

VYKAR. Well, we'll do what we have to, then get straight back to the ship.

JAYLIN. I suppose all this *is* worth it?

VYKAR. What do you mean?

JAYLIN. It just seems like we're taking a terrible risk to me.

VYKAR. What's the alternative? She's causing chaos, looking for this thing. *We* can do something about it.

JAYLIN. What? What can *we* do?

VYKAR. I don't know. Something! I'm going to ask her to reconsider. To take account of the misery she's caused. Ragana's like a black hole – she's collapsed in on herself and is pulling everyone else towards her. We all yearn for something! Every life form on every inhabited world *wants*. That's the engine, isn't it? The motive force that drives the universe. But none of us exists alone. What happens when *my* want impinges on you? Your... freedom? I have to moderate it, to... well, yes, maybe give it up. What's the alternative? That sort of monomania leaves worlds barren. Is that what we want? A universe of morbid, suffocating self-interest? One in which we're so turned in on ourselves that we can't see the abundance of wonder that's out there? No. I want to look up and see stars. I am a citizen of a universe in which everyone is illuminated by starlight.

RAGANA. Why, Vykar, how unsurprising – you're a socialist!

They spin round. In the doorway stands RAGANA – *the most feared being in the universe. Her deviousness and cruelty is the stuff of nightmares, her sense of style the stuff of legend. She wears a long white evening dress that could be considered timeless – though if you were to put a time to it, that time would be 1979.*

KOSLEY (*voice-over*). Commander, I did *try* to –

VYKAR slaps his communicator.

RAGANA *clicks her fingers.* VYKAR *and* JAYLIN *are hit by coloured beams of light that freeze them to the spot. In the confusion,* OLI, *still unseen by everyone, exits.*

VYKAR. Ragana!

JAYLIN. How did you know –

RAGANA. Oh, come! You think you could land here, unknown to me? Such naivety – it's almost charming in a way.

Why *are* you here?

She is met with silence.

Oh dear.

She gives a dismissive flick of her hand – and VYKAR *and* JAYLIN *twist in agony in their pillars of light.*

… two… three – with another desultory flick of her hand their torment subsides.

Perhaps now your tongues are loosened.

VYKAR. Go to hell, Ragana!

RAGANA *pantomimes a look of disappointment and slowly raises her hand to inflict a second bout.*

JAYLIN. No!

VYKAR (*reluctantly*). We came to rescue the President.

RAGANA. Well, I must say, you're not doing a very good job. No, it's more than that. You might have reached her but you know you'd never leave here alive. There's something else.

JAYLIN. We came to warn you!

RAGANA. Threats? How quaint.

VYKAR. No threat. Not of my making anyway. You're trying to take possession of a Shadow Ruby. You think that doing so will allow you to escape from your twilight dimension into ours.

RAGANA. You flatter yourself you know my mind.

VYKAR. But – don't you understand? A Shadow Ruby is impossible to possess! It burrows into your mind and turns your desire against yourself. It's a Paradox Mineral!

RAGANA. You think yourself advanced with your 'science'! I appeal to an older power! I channel forces beyond your comprehension!

VYKAR. The entire universe knows of your dark arts, Ragana. The filthy superstitions of a primitive age…

RAGANA. And yet…

She walks over to him. Strokes her hand across his face, down across his chest, flaunting her sensuality, her command…

I take it you have the Ruby?

JAYLIN. If *we* had it, why would we come here to warn *you* about it?

VYKAR. Jaylin, be quiet!

RAGANA. A fair point. So… You believe it to be here… Hmm.

VYKAR. Where is the President?

RAGANA. You're very demanding, Vykar.

VYKAR. I want to know she's safe!

RAGANA. Oh, she's safe.

Come!

A woman enters: as glamorous in her own way as RAGANA *but more subdued, her outfit more utilitarian –* THE PRESIDENT OF EARTH.

VYKAR. Madam President!

JAYLIN. Kayla!

Both VYKAR *and* RAGANA *register this informality with surprise.*

VYKAR. Madam President, are you –

PRESIDENT. Do not distress yourself, Vykar. I am well treated.

JAYLIN. She's constrained by some kind of force field.

RAGANA. Ah, you're a telepath. What interesting company you keep, Vykar.

VYKAR. Let her go!

RAGANA. She looks *very* well, does she not? Her clothes as bright as the day they were made. Her skin, unblemished. Her eyes…

With an effort, RAGANA *tears herself away.*

VYKAR. Why are you doing this, Ragana? What's it for?

RAGANA. The arrogance of that question!

Everything's clear to you, isn't it, Vykar? So sure of yourself as you speed through the galaxies, so righteous in your single-minded certainty. What is, *is*, to you. You've decided I'm wrong, so I am wrong. I wonder – is there ever a moment, between your escapades, for contemplation? Do you ever ask yourself who you are?

VYKAR. I know who I am. And I know what you are.

RAGANA. You know nothing!

I have heard the howling.

I see the void.

JAYLIN. Commander –

RAGANA. You have never known darkness.

JAYLIN. Commander!

A shimmering radiophonic noise.

VYKAR. What is it?

JAYLIN. Something's happening – !

An intense white light.

RAGANA. What trickery is this?

VYKAR. What is it? What can you –

They turn and see, in the remains of the doorway, OLI *– no, not* OLI*!* VOL*. He is dressed in silver boots, shorts, cuffs, and snood, and seems to radiate light. He has an unearthly calm about him.*

JAYLIN. Vol!

VYKAR. Vol?!

RAGANA. What is this?

VYKAR. Vol! What are you doing here? How – ?

VOL. This is where I am meant to be.

VYKAR. What? What do you mean? We thought you'd been –

VOL. The moment has come.

VYKAR. What 'moment'? What are you –

VOL. I was born in another dimension.

VYKAR. What?

JAYLIN. I always knew there was something about him.

VOL. I am here to serve destiny.

RAGANA. What *is* this?

VYKAR. Vol, I don't know what you're talking about but we can discuss this back on the ship –

VOL (*to* RAGANA). You desire the Shadow Ruby.

RAGANA. You have it?

VOL. You need it to fully enter this dimension. Possess the ruby and you become whole.

RAGANA. You Have It?

VOL. I have had a Shadow Ruby.

VYKAR. What?!

VOL. I have heard the howling. I have traversed the void. I have held the Shadow Ruby in my hands and felt the scorching darkness, felt it possess me, and repel me –

RAGANA. Where is it?

VOL. You have it.

RAGANA. What?

VOL. You have it.

RAGANA. Don't play games with me, boy!

VOL. You have it here now.

RAGANA flicks her hand and the room is enveloped in a green light, which, over the course of the next few lines, fades away except on the PRESIDENT, *where it turns a deep red. It is accompanied by an unearthly noise.* VYKAR *and* JAYLIN *have to shout to be heard. The* PRESIDENT *is in pain but stoic.*

RAGANA. No! You were searched, when brought here, for weaponry. Concealed technology. Anything injurious to my wellbeing. Or so I thought!

JAYLIN. What's she doing?

VYKAR. She didn't do her basic housekeeping! Rudimentary scans for lasers or explosives –

JAYLIN. So?

RAGANA. What a blind fool I've been…!

VYKAR. – but she didn't scan at a molecular level!

The PRESIDENT *is isolated in a beam of red light. Everyone's eyes are on her.*

JAYLIN. Why would she? What would that show?

With a flick of RAGANA's *wrist the light and sound stop. She looks at the* PRESIDENT.

RAGANA. Can it be that you – a mortal… So I thought…!

VOL. Yes.

RAGANA. Is this true?

JAYLIN. What does she –

VYKAR. Sssh!

RAGANA. You planted desire within me, and held me at arm's length. You are the fulfilment of the quest. *You* are the Shadow Ruby!

JAYLIN. What?

PRESIDENT. Yes. I carry that burden. A genetic quirk. A curse. But one I willingly bear if it keeps you from my people!

RAGANA. Burden? Do not speak to me of – ! I have laboured under the yoke of your allure since the dawn of time! I thought to have imprisoned you! *You* have imprisoned *me*!

PRESIDENT. And I rejoice to know it!

RAGANA. All this time… What might I have done, freed from the bonds of your enchantment? What might I have seen? Who might I have – been?

VYKAR. That's life.

RAGANA. That is *no* life!

VOL. This is the choice, Ragana. This is the moment. We cannot possess a Paradox Mineral. No one can. The light of the Shadow Ruby is released in the letting-go. Save yourself, as I saved myself.

A moment. They all look to her.

RAGANA. I want to live.

VOL. You live by letting go.

No answer.

VYKAR. Ragana, it's over.

Beat.

RAGANA. No.

VYKAR. What?

RAGANA. No.

This is a trick. Darkness is not answered by turning away
from the light –

VOL. This is no trick!

RAGANA. The howling is not silenced by screaming.

VOL. Ragana, I tell you –

RAGANA. You think, because we are from the same place, that
you can guide me? You *dare* to lecture me?

VOL. Ragana, I give you the only way to stay alive!

RAGANA. I am unmoved. I close the valves of my attention,
like stone!

*She closes her eyes. We hear a low rumble that grows in
strength.*

VYKAR. What's happening?

JAYLIN. She's activated a series of seismic tremors! She's
going to destroy the citadel!

VOL. You must go!

VYKAR. What about you?

VOL. I told you, Commander. I'm here for a reason.

JAYLIN. Vykar, come on, we've got to get out of here!

VYKAR (*into his wrist communicator*). Kosley! Stand by to
transmat four! Kosley!

A burst of static.

JAYLIN. The psychic disturbance is interfering with the signal!

VYKAR. Kosley! (*Gives up.*) We've got to get to the surface!

The sound of explosions and falling masonry.

Get the President! Vol, come on!

JAYLIN. But the force field – !

> VYKAR *hesitates, uncertain of what to do.* VOL *turns to them and holds up his hand.*

VOL. Take the President.

> VYKAR *realises that* VOL *is holding back the effects of the force field.*

VYKAR. You heard him! Get her out of here!

> VOL *is focused entirely on* RAGANA, *who is destroying the world by force of will.*

JAYLIN. Madame President! Kayla! Can you hear me? Are you all right? You must come with us!

> JAYLIN *takes the* PRESIDENT's *hand and leads her to the exit. They are all a little unsteady on their feet.*

PRESIDENT. Jaylin? Is it really you? What's going on?

JAYLIN. There's no time for that now! I'll explain later!

VYKAR. Vol!

VOL. Commander! You must go!

JAYLIN. Vykar, come on!

VYKAR. We can't leave him!

> VOL *walks slowly, with purpose, towards* RAGANA.

JAYLIN. Come on!

VYKAR. Vol! Let's get out of here!

VOL. No, Commander. This is where I have to be. Go.

> *Reluctantly, with a final look,* VYKAR *follows* JAYLIN *and the* PRESIDENT *out of the door. The noise of the dying world is now total.* VOL *reaches out and touches* RAGANA *on the shoulder.*

RAGANA. Stay your hand! I rue that you could slip my defences!

VOL. Defences? Ragana, I was invited in.

*He takes her by the shoulders and lies his head against her –
something approximating, but not quite, a hug.*

*Light builds on both of them. A small amount of lightweight
rocks and dust fall in the doorway.*

My gift to you. I release you. You're free.

A strange and terrible whooshing noise builds around them.

RAGANA. After so long? Can it be so? Free?

And now a sound – a sung note. Radiophonic. High.

She opens her eyes in panic.

What does that *mean*?

*The light that has been enveloping them blazes out, blinding
us.*

The Dark Sublime *theme comes screaming in!*

Scene Five

MARIANNE*'s flat.*

*From the bedroom, the sound of aggressive searching. From the
bedroom are thrown:*

A large, stringed puppet.

Three wellington boots.

An elaborate Mardi Gras headdress.

MARIANNE *enters from the bedroom, holding a yellowing
script.*

MARIANNE. 'I have laboured under the yoke of your allure
since the dawn of time. I thought to have imprisoned you.
You have imprisoned *me*!'

She sits down and starts to flick though the pages.

God in heaven.

He'll love it.

She lifts a white envelope from the table and goes to put the script inside it.

From the kitchen, the clink of glasses. A pop!

MARIANNE *looks over, startled. She puts the script and envelope on the table.*

KATE *comes from the kitchen, carrying two glasses of champagne.*

Where did you come from?

KATE. I've got a key.

MARIANNE. Oh.

What's this?

KATE. Champagne.

KATE *hands her a glass.*

MARIANNE. Have I died? Am I on *This Is Your Life*?

KATE. *This Is Your Life* finished years ago.

MARIANNE. Have they brought it back? Am I launching the new series?

KATE. Drink that.

Slightly self-consciously, they drink.

MARIANNE. I was a guest on *This Is Your Life* once. Eamonn Andrews surprised Liza Goddard opening a Bejam in Sutton Coldfi–

KATE. How was it?

MARIANNE. Great fun! I told the story about getting cramp while doing 'Chattanooga Choo-Choo' on *Give Us a Clue* –

KATE. How was the *convention*?

MARIANNE. Oh, that. Well, you know.

All right.

KATE. Were you a hit?

MARIANNE. Palpably so.

Yes.

It raised three thousand pounds.

KATE. Did it? That's impressive.

MARIANNE. Mmm.

Got a job from it, too. Some company that do these – audio dramas. The chap was there signing us all up. Like *The Afternoon Play*, but on CD. They sell them. People buy them.

I know!

KATE. And... Oli?

MARIANNE. Yes, he was there.

KATE. I know that. *He* invited *you*. Was he, um...?

How was he?

MARIANNE. Oh, he was...

Twenty-one.

KATE. Was he?

MARIANNE. It's a different world. You should hear him.

Ever since Diana died. Since then. Kids especially. They don't know any different. Opening up. Telling each other how they feel. It's just natural to them now. That's what *he's* like. It's all... to hand.

KATE. But they made a fuss?

MARIANNE. Oh, yes. For a brief weekend I was Queen of Walsall!

KATE. Listen.

   …

   I'm sorry.

MARIANNE. No, there are worse places. Radlett.

KATE. Marianne!

MARIANNE. Sorry.

KATE. I snapped and I didn't mean to and I don't want you to
   think that – I meant… More than I did.

MARIANNE. No, no, look, I –

KATE. I don't like not talking.

MARIANNE. No.

KATE. I just felt I needed to create a little space.

   I was feeling a bit –

   You are very, very dear to me.

   You're my best friend.

MARIANNE. Yes.

KATE. But – you were –

MARIANNE. I know. I know.

KATE. No. You were – being… unpleasant.

   MARIANNE *nods*.

   Whatever you felt, Suzanne didn't deserve that.

MARIANNE. No.

KATE. It got me thinking about everything and, you know –
   we… That first night. All those years ago! Coming over here,
   from Mike's – from the house. Coming away from Mike,
   I mean. That was – tough. And – you were lovely. To me.
   You were lovely to me.

MARIANNE. We were… lovely to each other.

KATE. I have… very fond memories of that night.

> I'd never… Well, you *know*, I'd never… before…! (*i.e. slept with a woman*.)

> And I'd never known what it was like to feel…

> To be told I was…

> We *did* have fun, and being with you was – You *weren't* like anyone I'd ever met. That was…!

> And, thinking back. Maybe I wasn't as… clear or considerate as I might have been. After.

> I think, the next morning, it was easy to… Well. Carry on.

> I'm as much to blame as…

MARIANNE. No. You weren't. You don't have to –

KATE. You've always made me feel – loved. I've always known –

> I've always known. And I should have… Before now. *Well* before now.

MARIANNE. Kate, please. It's fine. You don't have to say anything. I – know. I was… wrong. I –

KATE. Not 'wrong' –

MARIANNE. I – it was too much. I won't be again. I promise.

KATE. I want you to be happy.

> I do! What we have is – it's so strong, and… important. And anything more would be – something else. Wouldn't it? And I don't want that.

MARIANNE. No.

KATE. But I do want *this*.

MARIANNE. Yes.

KATE. Like this.

MARIANNE. Yes.

KATE. You understand, don't you?

MARIANNE. Yes. Yes, I do. I'm –

Sorry.

KATE. You don't have to say sorry.

MARIANNE. I do.

KATE. No, no, no.

MARIANNE. Yes.

KATE. No.

MARIANNE. Well.

Pause.

KATE. Marianne.

She puts her hand to her heart.

So much.

You and I…

She shakes her head – not saying 'no'. Having too much to say.

Yes?

MARIANNE *nods.*

Come here.

KATE *puts her head to* MARIANNE'*s. Strokes her.*

KATE *kisses her cheek.*

Hey.

Quietly, undemonstratively, MARIANNE *is crying.* KATE *looks for a tissue – she has none on her, and there are none to hand.* KATE *offers her sleeve.* MARIANNE *looks up and exhales a laugh at the absurdity of it – then dabs her eyes on* KATE'*s sleeve.*

There.

KATE *sits back. A pause.*

MARIANNE. Do you ever feel old?

KATE. No. And nor do you.

I'll top us up.

KATE *heads into the kitchen. As she goes she calls –*

I've given up the fags.

MARIANNE *takes a deep breath. Exhales. Closes her eyes.
We hear the same high radiophonic note as at the end of the
previous scene – then she opens her eyes and it snaps off.*

KATE *comes back in carrying the champagne bottle and a
couple of sheets of kitchen roll.*

I mean, it's early days but as long as you don't addle my
mind I might make a good fist of it.

She hands the kitchen roll to MARIANNE.

There you go.

MARIANNE *dabs her eyes with the kitchen roll. Blows her
nose.*

MARIANNE. Bloody hell. Well done, Suzanne.

KATE. No, it wasn't her. In a funny sort of a way I think it
was you.

MARIANNE. Me? Why me?

KATE *opens her mouth to reply, then –*

KATE. Oh, I don't know. Everything doesn't need an
explanation.

She tops up the glasses. Nods towards the script.

What's that?

She picks up the script, flicks through it.

MARIANNE. What? Oh, it's an old script from the show. Just
dug it out.

KATE. The stuff you keep hold of.

MARIANNE. It's a – ha! An – unfinished episode.

KATE. I could never make head nor tail of all this.

She puts the script back on the table.

Are you seeing him again?

MARIANNE. Oli? No, not –

She glances at the script.

No.

KATE. He'll be upset.

MARIANNE. He'll be all right. He'll be more than all right.

You can't really be friends with a fan.

On the table also is a small bag of sweets. MARIANNE *lifts the bag.*

Humbug?

KATE *carries on, without acknowledgement.*

KATE. Ah. Yes. Well, about that…

MARIANNE. Mmm?

KATE. I'm cooking on Friday night and I want you to come over. It'll be the three of us. You, me, and Suzanne.

MARIANNE. Yes. Great. I'd really like that.

KATE. Good. Good.

We'll start again, eh? What is it – 'reboot the franchise'?

MARIANNE. That'll be lovely.

KATE is oddly stilted, as though steeling herself.

KATE. Good. Well.

I'm glad you said yes. She's rather looking forward to it.

MARIANNE. Suzanne?

KATE. Yes. Now that I've promised her you're not going to be a psychopath – which you're *not* going to be!

MARIANNE. No, no!

KATE. She's going to give you another chance.

Because. It seems...

This is blood from a stone.

Back in the day...

No going back.

She was a... Big. Fan. Of...

Detonation.

Emmerdale.

So she's very keen to chat.

MARIANNE *meets* KATE*'s eye, throws her head back – and laughs!*

The Dark Sublime *theme comes screaming in!*

Lights out.

Looking up at the stars, I know quite well
That, for all they care, I can go to hell,
But on earth indifference is the least
We have to dread from man or beast.

How should we like it were stars to burn
With a passion for us we could not return?
If equal affection cannot be,
Let the more loving one be me.

Admirer as I think I am
Of stars that do not give a damn,
I cannot, now I see them, say
I missed one terribly all day.

Were all stars to disappear or die,
I should learn to look at an empty sky
And feel its total dark sublime,
Though this might take me a little time.

W. H. Auden

www.nickhernbooks.co.uk

facebook.com/nickhernbooks

twitter.com/nickhernbooks